ECONOMICS FOR INVESTMENT DECISION MAKERS WORKBOOK

CFA Institute is the premier association for investment professionals around the world, with over 117,000 members in 134 countries. Since 1963 the organization has developed and administered the renowned Chartered Financial Analyst® Program. With a rich history of leading the investment profession, CFA Institute has set the highest standards in ethics, education, and professional excellence within the global investment community, and is the foremost authority on investment profession conduct and practice.

Each book in the CFA Institute Investment Series is geared toward industry practitioners along with graduate-level finance students and covers the most important topics in the industry. The authors of these cutting-edge books are themselves industry professionals and academics and bring their wealth of knowledge and expertise to this series.

ECONOMICS FOR INVESTMENT DECISION MAKERS WORKBOOK

Micro, Macro, and International Economics

Christopher D. Piros, CFA

Jerald E. Pinto, CFA

WILEY

CONTENTS

PART I

LEARNING OUTCOMES, SUMMARY OVERVIEW, AND PRACTICE PROBLEMS

CHAPTER 1

DEMAND AND SUPPLY ANALYSIS: INTRODUCTION

LEARNING OUTCOMES

After completing this chapter, you will be able to do the following:

- Distinguish among types of markets.
- Explain the principles of demand and supply.
- Describe causes of shifts in and movements along demand and supply curves.
- Describe the process of aggregating demand and supply curves, the concept of equilibrium, and mechanisms by which markets achieve equilibrium.
- Distinguish between stable and unstable equilibria and identify instances of such equilibria.
- Calculate and interpret individual and aggregate demand and inverse demand and supply functions, and interpret individual and aggregate demand and supply curves.
- Calculate and interpret the amount of excess demand or excess supply associated with a nonequilibrium price.
- Describe the types of auctions and calculate the winning price(s) of an auction.
- Calculate and interpret consumer surplus, producer surplus, and total surplus.
- Analyze the effects of government regulation and intervention on demand and supply.
- Forecast the effect of the introduction and the removal of a market interference (e.g., a price floor or ceiling) on price and quantity.
- Calculate and interpret price, income, and cross-price elasticities of demand, and describe factors that affect each measure.

SUMMARY OVERVIEW

- The basic model of markets is the demand and supply model. The demand function represents buyers' behavior and can be depicted (in its inverse demand form) as a negatively sloped demand curve. The supply function represents sellers' behavior and can be depicted (in its inverse supply form) as a positively sloped supply curve. The interaction of buyers and sellers in a market results in equilibrium. Equilibrium exists when the highest price willingly paid by buyers is just equal to the lowest price willingly accepted by sellers.

- Goods markets are the interactions of consumers as buyers and firms as sellers of goods and services produced by firms and bought by households. Factor markets are the interactions of firms as buyers and households as sellers of land, labor, capital, and entrepreneurial risk-taking ability. Capital markets are used by firms to sell debt or equity to raise long-term capital to finance the production of goods and services.

- Demand and supply curves are drawn on the assumption that everything *except* the price of the good itself is held constant (an assumption known as ceteris paribus or "holding all other things constant"). When something other than price changes, the demand curve or the supply curve will shift relative to the other curve. This shift is referred to as a change in demand or supply, as opposed to quantity demanded or quantity supplied. A new equilibrium generally will be obtained at a different price and a different quantity than before. The market mechanism is the ability of prices to adjust to eliminate any excess demand or supply resulting from a shift in one or the other curve.

- If, at a given price, the quantity demanded exceeds the quantity supplied, there is excess demand and the price will rise. If, at a given price, the quantity supplied exceeds the quantity demanded, there is excess supply and the price will fall.

- Sometimes auctions are used to seek equilibrium prices. Common value auctions sell items that have the same value to all bidders, but bidders can only estimate that value before the auction is completed. Overly optimistic bidders overestimate the true value and end up paying a price greater than that value. This result is known as the winner's curse. Private value auctions sell items that (generally) have a unique subjective value for each bidder. Ascending price auctions use an auctioneer to call out ever-increasing prices until the last, highest bidder ultimately pays his or her bid price and buys the item. Descending price, or Dutch, auctions begin at a very high price and then reduce that price until one bidder is willing to buy at that price. Second price sealed-bid auctions are sometimes used to induce bidders to reveal their true reservation prices in private value auctions. Treasury notes and some other financial instruments are sold using a form of Dutch auction (called a single price auction) in which competitive and noncompetitive bids are arrayed in descending price (increasing yield) order. The winning bidders all pay the same price, but marginal bidders might not be able to fill their entire order at the market-clearing price.

- Markets that work freely can optimize society's welfare, as measured by consumer surplus and producer surplus. Consumer surplus is the difference between the total value to buyers and the total expenditure necessary to purchase a given amount. Producer surplus is the difference between the total revenue received by sellers from selling a given amount and the total variable cost of production of that amount. When equilibrium price is reached, total surplus is maximized.

- Sometimes, government policies interfere with the free working of markets. Examples include price ceilings, price floors, and specific taxes. Whenever the imposition of such a policy alters the free market equilibrium quantity (the quantity that maximizes total surplus), there is a redistribution of surplus between buyers and sellers; but there is also a reduction of total surplus, called deadweight loss. Other influences can result in an imbalance between demand and supply. Search costs are impediments in the ability of willing buyers and willing sellers to meet in a transaction. Brokers can add value if they reduce search costs and match buyers and sellers. In general, anything that improves information about the willingness of buyers and sellers to engage will reduce search costs and add value.

- Economists use a quantitative measure of sensitivity called elasticity. In general, elasticity is the ratio of the percentage change in the dependent variable to the percentage change in the independent variable of interest. Important specific elasticities include own-price elasticity of demand, income elasticity of demand, and cross-price elasticity of demand.

- Based on algebraic sign and magnitude of the various elasticities, goods can be classified into groups. If own-price elasticity of demand is less than 1 in absolute value, demand is called "inelastic"; it is called "elastic" if own-price elasticity of demand is greater than 1 in absolute value. Goods with positive income elasticity of demand are called normal goods, and those with negative income elasticity of demand are called inferior goods. Two goods with negative cross-price elasticity of demand—a drop in the price of one good causes an increase in demand for the other good—are called complements. Goods with positive cross-price elasticity of demand—a drop in the price of one good causes a decrease in demand for the other—are called substitutes.

- The relationship among own-price elasticity of demand, changes in price, and changes in total expenditure is as follows: If demand is elastic, a reduction in price results in an increase in total expenditure; if demand is inelastic, a reduction in price results in a decrease in total expenditure; if demand is unitary elastic, a change in price leaves total expenditure unchanged.

PRACTICE PROBLEMS[1]

1. Which of the following markets is *most* accurately characterized as a goods market? The market for:
   A. coats.
   B. sales clerks.
   C. cotton farmland.

2. The observation "As a price of a good falls, buyers buy more of it" is *best* known as:
   A. consumer surplus.
   B. the law of demand.
   C. the market mechanism.

3. Two-dimensional demand and supply curves are drawn under which of the following assumptions?
   A. Own price is held constant.
   B. All variables but quantity are held constant.
   C. All variables but own price and quantity are held constant.

4. The slope of a supply curve is *most* often:
   A. zero.
   B. positive.
   C. negative.

5. Assume the following equation:

$$Q_x^s = -4 + \tfrac{1}{2}P_x - 2W$$

---

[1]These practice problems were written by William Akmentins, CFA (Dallas, Texas, USA).

where Q_x^s is the quantity of good X supplied, P_x is the price of good X, and W is the wage rate paid to laborers. If the wage rate is 11, the vertical intercept on a graph depicting the supply curve is *closest* to:

A. −26.

B. −4.

C. 52.

6. Movement along the demand curve for good X occurs due to a change in:

   A. income.

   B. the price of good X.

   C. the price of a substitute for good X.

The following information relates to Questions 7 through 9.

A producer's supply function is given by the equation:

$$Q_s^s = -55 + 26P_s + 1.3P_a$$

where Q_s^s is the quantity of steel supplied by the market, P_s is the per-unit price of steel, and P_a is the per-unit price of aluminum.

7. If the price of aluminum rises, what happens to the steel producer's supply curve? The supply curve:

   A. shifts to the left.

   B. shifts to the right.

   C. remains unchanged.

8. If the unit price of aluminum is 10, the slope of the supply curve is *closest* to:

   A. 0.04.

   B. 1.30.

   C. 26.00.

9. Assume the supply side of the market consists of exactly five identical sellers. If the unit price of aluminum is 20, which equation is *closest* to the expression for the market inverse supply function?

   A. $P_s = 9.6 + 0.04Q_s^s$

   B. $P_s = 1.1 + 0.008Q_s^s$

   C. $Q_s^s = -145 + 130P_s$

10. Which of the following statements about market equilibrium is *most* accurate?

    A. The difference between quantity demanded and quantity supplied is zero.

    B. The demand curve is negatively sloped and the supply curve is positively sloped.

    C. For any given pair of market demand and supply curves, only one equilibrium point can exist.

11. Which of the following statements *best* characterizes the market mechanism for attaining equilibrium?
    A. Excess supply causes prices to fall.
    B. Excess demand causes prices to fall.
    C. The demand and supply curves shift to reach equilibrium.

12. An auction in which the auctioneer starts at a high price and then lowers the price in increments until there is a willing buyer is *best* called a:
    A. Dutch auction.
    B. Vickery auction.
    C. private value auction.

13. Which statement is *most likely* to be true in a single price U.S. Treasury bill auction?
    A. Only some noncompetitive bids would be filled.
    B. Bidders at the highest winning yield may get only a portion of their orders filled.
    C. All bidders at a yield higher than the winning bid would get their entire orders filled.

14. The winner's curse in common value auctions is *best* described as the winning bidder paying:
    A. more than the value of the asset.
    B. a price not equal to one's own bid.
    C. more than intended prior to bidding.

15. A wireless phone manufacturer introduced a next-generation phone that received a high level of positive publicity. Despite running several high-speed production assembly lines, the manufacturer is still falling short in meeting demand for the phone nine months after introduction. Which of the following statements is the *most* plausible explanation for the demand/supply imbalance?
    A. The phone price is low relative to the equilibrium price.
    B. Competitors introduced next-generation phones at a similar price.
    C. Consumer incomes grew faster than the manufacturer anticipated.

16. A per-unit tax on items sold that is paid by the seller will *most likely* result in the:
    A. supply curve shifting vertically upward.
    B. demand curve shifting vertically upward.
    C. demand curve shifting vertically downward.

17. Which of the following *most* accurately and completely describes a deadweight loss?
    A. A transfer of surplus from one party to another
    B. A reduction in either the buyer's or the seller's surplus
    C. A reduction in total surplus resulting from market interference

18. If an excise tax is paid by the buyer instead of the seller, which of the following statements is *most likely* to be true?
    A. The price paid will be higher than if the seller had paid the tax.
    B. The price received will be lower than if the seller had paid the tax.
    C. The price received will be the same as if the seller had paid the tax.

19. A quota on an imported good below the market-clearing quantity will *most likely* lead to which of the following effects?
   A. The supply curve shifts upward.
   B. The demand curve shifts upward.
   C. Some of the buyer's surplus transfers to the seller.

20. Assume a market demand function is given by the equation:

$$Q^d = 50 - 0.75P$$

where Q^d is the quantity demanded and P is the price. If P equals 10, the value of the consumer surplus is *closest* to:
   A. 67.
   B. 1,205.
   C. 1,667.

21. Which of the following *best* describes producer surplus?
   A. Revenue minus variable costs
   B. Revenue minus variable plus fixed costs
   C. The area above the supply curve and beneath the demand curve and to the left of the equilibrium point

22. Assume a market supply function is given by the equation

$$Q_s = -7 + 0.6P$$

where Q_s is the quantity supplied and P is the price. If P equals 15, the value of the producer surplus is *closest* to:
   A. 3.3.
   B. 41.0.
   C. 67.5.

The following information relates to Questions 23 through 25.

The market demand function for four-year private universities is given by the equation:

$$Q_{pr}^d = 84 - 3.1P_{pr} + 0.8I + 0.9P_{pu}$$

where Q_{pr}^d is the number of applicants to private universities per year in thousands, P_{pr} is the average price of private universities (in thousands of USD), I is the household monthly income (in thousands of USD), and P_{pu} is the average price of public (government-supported) universities (in thousands of USD). Assume that P_{pr} is equal to 38, I is equal to 100, and P_{pu} is equal to 18.

23. The price elasticity of demand for private universities is *closest* to:
   A. −3.1.
   B. −1.9.
   C. 0.6.

24. The income elasticity of demand for private universities is *closest* to:
    A. 0.5.
    B. 0.8.
    C. 1.3.

25. The cross-price elasticity of demand for private universities with respect to the average price of public universities is *closest* to:
    A. 0.3.
    B. 3.1.
    C. 3.9.

26. If the cross-price elasticity between two goods is negative, the two goods are classified as:
    A. normal.
    B. substitutes.
    C. complements.

CHAPTER 2

DEMAND AND SUPPLY ANALYSIS: CONSUMER DEMAND

LEARNING OUTCOMES

After completing this chapter, you will be able to do the following:

- Describe consumer choice theory and utility theory.
- Describe the use of indifference curves, opportunity sets, and budget constraints in decision making.
- Calculate and interpret a budget constraint.
- Determine a consumer's equilibrium bundle of goods based on utility analysis.
- Compare substitution and income effects.
- Distinguish between normal goods and inferior goods, and explain Giffen goods and Veblen goods in this context.

SUMMARY OVERVIEW

- Consumer choice theory is the branch of microeconomics that relates consumer demand curves to consumer preferences. Utility theory is a quantitative model of consumer preferences and is based on a set of axioms (assumptions that are assumed to be true). If consumer preferences are complete, transitive, and insatiable, those preferences can be represented by an ordinal utility function and depicted by a set of indifference curves that are generally negatively sloped, are convex from below, and do not cross for a given consumer.
- A consumer's relative strength of preferences can be inferred from his marginal rate of substitution of good X for good Y (MRS_{XY}), which is the rate at which the consumer is willing to sacrifice good Y to obtain an additional small increment of good X. If two consumers have different marginal rates of substitution, they can both benefit from the voluntary exchange of one good for the other.
- A consumer's attainable consumption options are determined by her income and the prices of the goods she must purchase to consume. The set of options available is bounded by the budget constraint, a negatively sloped linear relationship that shows the highest quantity of one good that can be purchased for any given amount of the other good being bought.

- Analogous to the consumer's consumption opportunity set are, respectively, the production opportunity set and the investment opportunity set. A company's production opportunity set represents the greatest quantity of one product that a company can produce for any given amount of the other good it produces. The investment opportunity set represents the highest return an investor can expect for any given amount of risk undertaken.
- Consumer equilibrium is obtained when utility is maximized, subject to the budget constraint, generally depicted as a tangency between the highest attainable indifference curve and the fixed budget constraint. At that tangency, the MRS_{XY} is just equal to the two goods' price ratio, P_X/P_Y—or that bundle such that the rate at which the consumer is just willing to sacrifice good Y for good X is equal to the rate at which, based on prices, she must sacrifice good Y for good X.
- If the consumer's income and the price of all other goods are held constant and the price of good X is varied, the set of consumer equilibria that results will yield that consumer's demand curve for good X. In general, we expect the demand curve to have a negative slope (the law of demand) because of two influences: income and substitution effects of a decrease in price. Normal goods have a negatively sloped demand curve. For normal goods, income and substitution effects reinforce one another. However, for inferior goods, the income effect offsets part or all of the substitution effect. In the case of the Giffen good, the income effect of this very inferior good overwhelms the substitution effect, resulting in a positively sloped demand curve.
- In accepted microeconomic consumer theory, the consumer is assumed to be able to judge the value of any given bundle of goods without knowing anything about their prices. Then, constrained by income and prices, the consumer is assumed to be able to choose the optimal bundle of goods that is in the set of available options. It is possible to conceive of a situation in which the consumer cannot truly value a good until the price is known. In these Veblen goods, the price is used by the consumer to signal the consumer's status in society. Thus, to some extent, the higher the price of the good, the more value it offers to the consumer. In the extreme case, this could possibly result in a positively sloped demand curve. This result is similar to a Giffen good, but the two goods are fundamentally different.

PRACTICE PROBLEMS[1]

1. A child indicates that she prefers going to the zoo over the park and prefers going to the beach over the zoo. When given the choice between the park and the beach, she chooses the park. Which of the following assumptions of consumer preference theory is she *most likely* violating?
   A. Nonsatiation
   B. Complete preferences
   C. Transitive preferences

2. Which of the following ranking systems *best* describes consumer preferences within a utility function?
   A. Util
   B. Ordinal
   C. Cardinal

[1]These practice problems were written by William Akmentins, CFA (Dallas, Texas, USA).

3. Which of the following statements *best* explains why indifference curves are generally convex as viewed from the origin?
   A. The assumption of nonsatiation results in convex indifference curves.
   B. The marginal rate of substitution of one good for another remains constant along an indifference curve.
   C. The marginal utility gained from one additional unit of a good versus another diminishes the more one has of the first good.

4. If a consumer's marginal rate of substitution of good X for good Y (MRS_{XY}) is equal to 2, then the:
   A. consumer is willing to give up two units of X for one unit of Y.
   B. slope of a line tangent to the indifference curve at that point is 2.
   C. slope of a line tangent to the indifference curve at that point is -2.

5. In the case of two goods, x and y, which of the following statements is *most likely* true? Maximum utility is achieved:
   A. along the highest indifference curve below the budget constraint line.
   B. at the tangency between the highest attainable indifference curve and the budget constraint line.
   C. when the marginal rate of substitution is equal to the ratio of the price of good y to the price of good x.

6. In the case of a normal good with a decrease in its own price, which of the following statements is *most likely* true?
   A. Both the substitution effect and the income effect lead to an increase in the quantity purchased.
   B. The substitution effect leads to an increase in the quantity purchased, while the income effect has no impact.
   C. The substitution effect leads to an increase in the quantity purchased, while the income effect leads to a decrease.

7. For a Giffen good, the:
   A. demand curve is positively sloped.
   B. substitution effect overwhelms the income effect.
   C. income and substitution effects are in the same direction.

8. Which of the following statements *best* illustrates the difference between a Giffen good and a Veblen good?
   A. The Giffen good alone is an inferior good.
   B. Their substitution effects are in opposite directions.
   C. The Veblen good alone has a positively sloped demand curve.

CHAPTER 3

DEMAND AND SUPPLY ANALYSIS: THE FIRM

LEARNING OUTCOMES

After completing this chapter, you will be able to do the following:

- Calculate, interpret, and compare accounting profit, economic profit, normal profit, and economic rent.
- Calculate, interpret, and compare total, average, and marginal revenue.
- Describe the firm's factors of production.
- Calculate and interpret total, average, marginal, fixed, and variable costs.
- Determine and describe breakeven and shutdown points of production.
- Explain how economies of scale and diseconomies of scale affect costs.
- Describe approaches to determining the profit-maximizing level of output.
- Distinguish between short-run and long-run profit maximization.
- Distinguish among decreasing-cost, constant-cost, and increasing-cost industries and describe the long-run supply of each.
- Calculate and interpret total, marginal, and average product of labor.
- Describe the phenomenon of diminishing marginal returns, and calculate and interpret the profit-maximizing utilization level of an input.
- Determine the optimal combination of resources that minimizes cost.

SUMMARY OVERVIEW

- The two major concepts of profits are accounting profit and economic profit. Economic profit equals accounting profit minus implicit opportunity costs not included in accounting costs. Profit in the theory of the firm refers to economic profit.
- Normal profit is an economic profit of zero. A firm earning a normal profit is earning just enough to cover the explicit and implicit costs of resources used in running the firm, including, most importantly for publicly traded corporations, debt and equity capital.
- Economic profit is a residual value in excess of normal profit and results from access to positive NPV investment opportunities.
- The factors of production are the inputs to the production of goods and services and include land, labor, capital, and materials.

- Profit maximization occurs at the following points:
  - Where the difference between total revenue and total costs is the greatest.
  - Where marginal revenue equals marginal cost.
  - Where marginal revenue product equals the resource cost for each type of input.
- When total costs exceed total revenue, loss minimization occurs where the difference between total costs and total revenue is the least.
- In the long run, all inputs to the firm are variable, which expands profit potential and the number of cost structures available to the firm.
- Under perfect competition, long-run profit maximization occurs at the minimum point of the firm's long-run average total cost curve.
- In an economic loss situation, a firm can operate in the short run if total revenue covers variable cost but is inadequate to cover fixed cost; however, in the long run, the firm will exit the market if fixed costs are not covered in full.
- In an economic loss situation, a firm shuts down in the short run if total revenue does not cover variable cost in full, and eventually exits the market if the shortfall is not reversed.
- Economies of scale lead to lower average total cost; diseconomies of scale lead to higher average total cost.
- A firm's production function defines the relationship between total product and inputs.
- Average product and marginal product, which are derived from total product, are key measures of a firm's productivity.
- Increases in productivity reduce business costs and enhance profitability.
- An industry supply curve that is positively sloped in the long run will increase production costs to the firm. An industry supply curve that is negatively sloped in the long run will decrease production costs to the firm.
- In the short run, assuming constant resource prices, increasing marginal returns reduce the marginal costs of production, and decreasing marginal returns increase the marginal costs of production.

PRACTICE PROBLEMS[1]

1. Normal profit is *best* described as:
   A. zero economic profit.
   B. total revenue minus all explicit costs.
   C. the sum of accounting profit plus economic profit.

2. A firm supplying a commodity product in the marketplace is *most likely* to receive economic rent if:
   A. demand increases for the commodity and supply is elastic.
   B. demand increases for the commodity and supply is inelastic.
   C. supply increases for the commodity and demand is inelastic.

3. Entrepreneurs are *most likely* to receive payment or compensation in the form of:
   A. rent.
   B. profit.
   C. wages.

[1]These practice problems were developed by Christopher Anderson, CFA (Lawrence, Kansas, USA).

4. The marketing director for a Swiss specialty equipment manufacturer estimates the firm can sell 200 units and earn total revenue of CHF500,000. However, if 250 units are sold, revenue will total CHF600,000. The marginal revenue per unit associated with marketing 250 units instead of 200 units is *closest* to:
   A. CHF2,000.
   B. CHF2,400.
   C. CHF2,500.

5. An agricultural firm operating in a perfectly competitive market supplies wheat to manufacturers of consumer food products and animal feeds. If the firm were able to expand its production and unit sales by 10 percent, the *most likely* result would be:
   A. a 10 percent increase in total revenue.
   B. a 10 percent increase in average revenue.
   C. an increase in total revenue of less than 10 percent.

6. An operator of a ski resort is considering offering price reductions on weekday ski passes. At the normal price of €50 per day, 300 customers are expected to buy passes each weekday. At a discounted price of €40 per day, 450 customers are expected to buy passes each weekday. The marginal revenue per customer earned from offering the discounted price is *closest* to:
   A. €20.
   B. €40.
   C. €50.

7. The marginal revenue per unit sold for a firm doing business under conditions of perfect competition will *most likely* be:
   A. equal to average revenue.
   B. less than average revenue.
   C. greater than average revenue.

The following information relates to Questions 8 through 10.

A firm's director of operations gathers the following information about the firm's cost structure at different levels of output:

Exhibit A

Quantity (Q)	Total Fixed Cost (TFC)	Total Variable Cost (TVC)
0	200	0
1	200	100
2	200	150
3	200	200
4	200	240
5	200	320

8. Refer to the data in Exhibit A. When quantity produced is equal to four units, the average fixed cost (*AFC*) is *closest* to:
   A. 50.
   B. 60.
   C. 110.

9. Refer to the data in Exhibit A. When the firm increases production from four to five units, the marginal cost (*MC*) is *closest* to:
   A. 40.
   B. 64.
   C. 80.

10. Refer to the data in Exhibit A. The level of unit production resulting in the lowest average total cost (*ATC*) is *closest* to:
    A. 3.
    B. 4.
    C. 5.

11. The short-term breakeven point of production for a firm operating under perfect competition will *most likely* occur when:
    A. price is equal to average total cost.
    B. marginal revenue is equal to marginal cost.
    C. marginal revenue is equal to average variable costs.

12. The short-term shutdown point of production for a firm operating under perfect competition will *most likely* occur when:
    A. price is equal to average total cost.
    B. marginal revenue is equal to marginal cost.
    C. marginal revenue is less than average variable costs.

13. When total revenue is greater than total variable costs but less than total costs, in the short term a firm will *most likely*:
    A. exit the market.
    B. stay in the market.
    C. shut down production.

14. A profit maximum is *least likely* to occur when:
    A. average total cost is minimized.
    B. marginal revenue equals marginal cost.
    C. the difference between total revenue and total cost is maximized.

15. A firm that increases its quantity produced without any change in per-unit cost is experiencing:
    A. economies of scale.
    B. diseconomies of scale.
    C. constant returns to scale.

16. A firm is operating beyond minimum efficient scale in a perfectly competitive industry. To maintain long-term viability, the *most likely* course of action for the firm is to:
    A. operate at the current level of production.
    B. increase its level of production to gain economies of scale.
    C. decrease its level of production to the minimum point on the long-run average total cost curve.

17. Under conditions of perfect competition, in the long run firms will *most likely* earn:
    A. normal profits.
    B. positive economic profits.
    C. negative economic profits.

18. A firm engages in the development and extraction of oil and gas, the supply of which is price inelastic. The *most likely* equilibrium response in the long run to an increase in the demand for petroleum is that oil prices:
    A. increase, and extraction costs per barrel fall.
    B. increase, and extraction costs per barrel rise.
    C. remain constant, and extraction costs per barrel remain constant.

19. A firm develops and markets consumer electronic devices in a perfectly competitive, decreasing-cost industry. The firm's products have grown in popularity. The *most likely* equilibrium response in the long run to rising demand for such devices is for selling prices to:
    A. fall and per-unit production costs to decrease.
    B. rise and per-unit production costs to decrease.
    C. remain constant and per-unit production costs to remain constant.

The following information relates to Questions 20 and 21.

The manager of a small manufacturing firm gathers the following information about the firm's labor utilization and production:

Exhibit B

Labor (L)	Total Product (TP)
0	0
1	150
2	320
3	510
4	660
5	800

20. Refer to the data in Exhibit B. The number of workers resulting in the highest level of average product of labor is *closest* to:
    A. 3.
    B. 4.
    C. 5.

21. Refer to the data in Exhibit B. The marginal product of labor demonstrates increasing returns for the firm if the number of workers is *closest* to but not more than:
    A. 2.
    B. 3.
    C. 4.

22. A firm experiencing an increase in the marginal product of labor employed would *most likely*:
    A. allow an increased number of workers to specialize and become more adept at their individual functions.
    B. find that an increase in workers cannot be efficiently matched by other inputs that are fixed, such as property, plant, and equipment.
    C. find that the supply of skilled workers is limited, and additional workers lack essential skills and aptitudes possessed by the current workforce.

23. For a manufacturing company to achieve the most efficient combination of labor and capital and therefore to minimize total costs for a desired level of output, it will *most likely* attempt to equalize the:
    A. average product of labor to the average product of capital.
    B. marginal product per unit of labor to the marginal product per unit of capital.
    C. marginal product obtained per dollar spent on labor to the marginal product per dollar spent on capital.

24. A firm will expand production by 200 units and must hire at least one additional worker. The marginal product per day for one additional unskilled worker is 100 units, and for one additional skilled worker it is 200 units. Wages per day are $200 for an unskilled worker and $450 for a skilled worker. The firm will *most likely* minimize costs at the higher level of production by hiring:
    A. one additional skilled worker.
    B. two additional unskilled workers.
    C. either a skilled worker or two unskilled workers.

25. A Mexican firm employs unskilled, semiskilled, and skilled labor in a cost-minimizing mix at its manufacturing plant. The marginal product of unskilled labor is considerably lower than semiskilled and skilled labor, but the equilibrium wage for unskilled labor is only 300 pesos per day. The government passes a law that mandates a minimum wage of 400 pesos per day. Equilibrium wages for semiskilled and skilled labor exceed this minimum wage and therefore are not affected by the new law. The firm will *most likely* respond to the imposition of the minimum wage law by:
    A. employing more unskilled workers at its plant.
    B. employing fewer unskilled workers at its plant.
    C. keeping the mix of unskilled, semiskilled, and skilled workers the same.

The following information relates to Questions 26 and 27.

A firm produces handcrafted wooden chairs, employing both skilled craftspersons and automated equipment in its plant. The selling price of a chair is €100. A craftsperson earns €900 per week and can produce 10 chairs per week. Automated equipment leased for €800 per week also can produce 10 chairs per week.

26. The marginal revenue product (per week) of hiring an additional craftsperson is *closest* to:
    A. €100.
    B. €900.
    C. €1,000.

27. The firm would like to increase weekly output by 50 chairs. The firm would *most likely* enhance profits by:
    A. hiring additional craftspersons.
    B. leasing additional automated equipment.
    C. leasing additional automated equipment and hiring additional craftspersons in equal proportion.

CHAPTER 4

THE FIRM AND MARKET STRUCTURES

LEARNING OUTCOMES

After completing this chapter, you will be able to do the following:

- Describe the characteristics of perfect competition, monopolistic competition, oligopoly, and pure monopoly.
- Explain the relationships among price, marginal revenue, marginal cost, economic profit, and the elasticity of demand under each market structure.
- Describe the firm's supply function under each market structure.
- Describe and determine the optimal price and output for firms under each market structure.
- Explain factors affecting long-run equilibrium under each market structure.
- Describe pricing strategy under each market structure.
- Describe the use and limitations of concentration measures in identifying the various forms of market structure.
- Identify the type of market structure a firm is operating within.

SUMMARY OVERVIEW

- Economic market structures can be grouped into four categories: perfect competition, monopolistic competition, oligopoly, and monopoly.
- The categories differ because of the following characteristics: The number of producers is many in perfect and monopolistic competition, few in oligopoly, and one in monopoly. The degree of product differentiation, the pricing power of the producer, the barriers to entry of new producers, and the level of nonprice competition (e.g., advertising) are all low in perfect competition, moderate in monopolistic competition, high in oligopoly, and generally highest in monopoly.
- A financial analyst must understand the characteristics of market structures in order to better forecast a firm's future profit stream.
- The optimal marginal revenue equals marginal cost. However, only in perfect competition does the marginal revenue equal price. In the remaining structures, price generally exceeds marginal revenue because a firm can sell more units only by reducing the per-unit price.

- The quantity sold is highest in perfect competition. The price in perfect competition is usually lowest, but this depends on factors such as demand elasticity and increasing returns to scale (which may reduce the producer's marginal cost). Monopolists, oligopolists, and producers in monopolistic competition attempt to differentiate their products so they can charge higher prices.
- Typically, monopolists sell a smaller quantity at a higher price. Investors may benefit from being shareholders of monopolistic firms that have large margins and substantial positive cash flows.
- Competitive firms do not earn economic profit. There will be a market compensation for the rental of capital and of management services, but the lack of pricing power implies that there will be no extra margins.
- While in the short run firms in any market structure can have economic profits, the more competitive a market is and the lower the barriers to entry, the faster the extra profits will fade. In the long run, new entrants shrink margins and push the least efficient firms out of the market.
- Oligopoly is characterized by the importance of strategic behavior. Firms can change the price, quantity, quality, and advertisement of the product to gain an advantage over their competitors. Several types of equilibrium (e.g., Nash, Cournot, kinked demand curve) may occur that affect the likelihood of each of the incumbents (and potential entrants in the long run) having economic profits. Price wars may be started to force weaker competitors to abandon the market.
- Measuring market power is complicated. Ideally, econometric estimates of the elasticity of demand and supply should be computed. However, because of the lack of reliable data and the fact that elasticity changes over time (so that past data may not apply to the current situation), regulators and economists often use simpler measures. The concentration ratio is simple, but the HHI, with little more computation required, often produces a better figure for decision making.

PRACTICE PROBLEMS[1]

1. A market structure characterized by many sellers with each having some pricing power and product differentiation is *best* described as:
   A. oligopoly.
   B. perfect competition.
   C. monopolistic competition.

2. A market structure with relatively few sellers of a homogeneous or standardized product is *best* described as:
   A. oligopoly.
   B. monopoly.
   C. perfect competition.

3. Market competitors are *least likely* to use advertising as a tool of differentiation in an industry structure identified as:
   A. monopoly.
   B. perfect competition.
   C. monopolistic competition.

---

[1]These practice problems were written by Tim Mahoney, CFA (Greenville, Rhode Island, USA).

4. Upsilon Natural Gas, Inc. is a monopoly enjoying very high barriers to entry. Its marginal cost is $40 and its average cost is $70. A recent market study has determined that the price elasticity of demand is 1.5. The company will *most likely* set its price at:
   A. $40.
   B. $70.
   C. $120.

5. The demand schedule in a perfectly competitive market is given by $P = 93 - 1.5Q$ (for $Q \le 62$) and the long-run cost structure of each company is:

Total cost:	$256 + 2Q + 4Q^2$
Average cost:	$256/Q + 2 + 4Q$
Marginal cost:	$2 + 8Q$

   New companies will enter the market at any price greater than:
   A. 8.
   B. 66.
   C. 81.

6. Companies *most likely* have a well-defined supply function when the market structure is:
   A. oligopoly.
   B. perfect competition.
   C. monopolistic competition.

7. Aquarius, Inc. is the dominant company and the price leader in its market. One of the other companies in the market attempts to gain market share by undercutting the price set by Aquarius. The market share of Aquarius will *most likely*:
   A. increase.
   B. decrease.
   C. stay the same.

8. SigmaSoft and ThetaTech are the dominant makers of computer system software. The market has two components: a large mass-market component in which demand is price sensitive, and a smaller performance-oriented component in which demand is much less price sensitive. SigmaSoft's product is considered to be technically superior. Each company can choose one of two strategies:

   1. *Open architecture (Open):* Mass-market focus allowing other software vendors to develop products for its platform.
   2. *Proprietary (Prop):* Allowing only its own software applications to run on its platform.

Depending on the strategy each company selects, their profits would be:

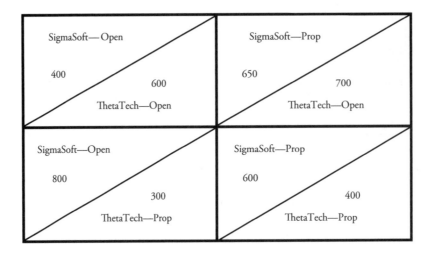

The Nash equilibrium for these companies is:
A. proprietary for SigmaSoft and proprietary for ThetaTech.
B. open architecture for SigmaSoft and proprietary for ThetaTech.
C. proprietary for SigmaSoft and open architecture for ThetaTech.

9. A company doing business in a monopolistically competitive market will *most likely* maximize profits when its output quantity is set such that:
A. average cost is minimized.
B. marginal revenue equals average cost.
C. marginal revenue equals marginal cost.

10. Oligopolistic pricing strategy *most likely* results in a demand curve that is:
A. kinked.
B. vertical.
C. horizontal.

11. Collusion is *less likely* in a market when:
A. the product is homogeneous.
B. companies have similar market shares.
C. the cost structures of companies are similar.

12. If companies earn economic profits in a perfectly competitive market, over the long run the supply curve will *most likely*:
A. shift to the left.
B. shift to the right.
C. remain unchanged.

13. Over time, the market share of the dominant company in an oligopolistic market will *most likely*:
    A. increase.
    B. decrease.
    C. remain the same.

14. A government entity that regulates an authorized monopoly will *most likely* base regulated prices on:
    A. marginal cost.
    B. long-run average cost.
    C. first-degree price discrimination.

15. An analyst gathers the following market share data for an industry:

Company	Sales (in millions of €)
ABC	300
Brown	250
Coral	200
Delta	150
Erie	100
All others	50

The industry's four-company concentration ratio is *closest* to:
A. 71 percent.
B. 86 percent.
C. 95 percent.

16. An analyst gathers the following market share data for an industry comprised of five companies:

Company	Market Share (%)
Zeta	35
Yusef	25
Xenon	20
Waters	10
Vlastos	10

The industry's three-firm Herfindahl-Hirschman index is *closest* to:
A. 0.185.
B. 0.225.
C. 0.235.

17. One disadvantage of the Herfindahl-Hirschman index is that the index:
    A. is difficult to compute.
    B. fails to reflect low barriers to entry.
    C. fails to reflect the effect of mergers in the industry.

18. In an industry consisting of three companies that are small-scale manufacturers of an easily replicable product unprotected by brand recognition or patents, the *most* representative model of company behavior is:
    A. oligopoly.
    B. perfect competition.
    C. monopolistic competition.

19. Deep River Manufacturing is one of many companies in an industry making a food product. Deep River units are identical up to the point they are labeled. Deep River produces its labeled brand, which sells for $2.20 per unit, and house brands for seven different grocery chains that sell for $2.00 per unit. Each grocery chain sells both the Deep River brand and its house brand. The *best* characterization of Deep River's market is:
    A. oligopoly.
    B. perfect competition.
    C. monopolistic competition.

CHAPTER 5

AGGREGATE OUTPUT, PRICES, AND ECONOMIC GROWTH

LEARNING OUTCOMES

After completing this chapter, you will be able to do the following:

- Calculate and explain gross domestic product (GDP) using expenditure and income approaches.
- Compare the sum-of-value-added and value-of-final-output methods of calculating GDP.
- Compare nominal and real GDP, and calculate and interpret the GDP deflator.
- Compare GDP, national income, personal income, and personal disposable income.
- Explain the fundamental relationship among saving, investment, the fiscal balance, and the trade balance.
- Explain the investment–saving (IS) and liquidity preference–money supply (LM) curves and how they combine to generate the aggregate demand curve.
- Explain the aggregate supply curve in the short run and the long run.
- Explain the causes of movements along and shifts in the aggregate demand and supply curves.
- Describe how fluctuations in aggregate demand and aggregate supply cause short-run changes in the economy and the business cycle.
- Explain how a short-run macroeconomic equilibrium may occur at a level above or below full employment.
- Analyze the effect of combined changes in aggregate supply and demand on the economy.
- Describe the sources, measurement, and sustainability of economic growth.
- Describe the production function approach to analyzing the sources of economic growth.
- Distinguish between input growth and growth of total factor productivity as components of economic growth.

SUMMARY OVERVIEW

- GDP is the market value of all final goods and services produced within a country in a given time period.

- GDP can be valued by looking at either the total amount spent on goods and services produced in the economy or the income generated in producing those goods and services.
- GDP counts only final purchases of newly produced goods and services during the current time period. Transfer payments and capital gains are excluded from GDP.
- With the exception of owner-occupied housing and government services, which are estimated at imputed values, GDP includes only goods and services that are valued by being sold in the market.
- Intermediate goods are excluded from GDP in order to avoid double counting.
- GDP can be measured either from the value of final output or by summing the value added at each stage of the production and distribution process. The sum of the value added by each stage is equal to the final selling price of the good.
- Nominal GDP is the value of production using the prices of the current year. Real GDP measures production using the constant prices of a base year. The GDP deflator equals the ratio of nominal GDP to real GDP.
- Households earn income in exchange for providing—directly or indirectly through ownership of businesses—the factors of production (labor, capital, natural resources including land). From this income, they consume, save, and pay net taxes.
- Businesses produce most of the economy's output/income and invest to maintain and expand productive capacity. Companies retain some earnings but pay out most of their revenue as income to the household sector and as taxes to the government.
- The government sector collects taxes from households and businesses and purchases goods and services from the private business sector.
- Foreign trade consists of exports and imports. The difference between the two is net exports. If net exports are positive, then the country spends less than it earns; if exports are negative, it spends more than it earns. Net exports are balanced by accumulation of either claims on the rest of the world (net exports > 0) or obligations to the rest of the world (net exports < 0).
- Capital markets provide a link between saving and investment in the economy.
- From the expenditure side, GDP includes personal consumption (C), gross private domestic investment (I), government spending (G), and net exports ($X - M$).
- The major categories of expenditure are often broken down into subcategories. Gross private domestic investment includes both investment in fixed assets (plant and equipment) and the change in inventories. In some countries, government investment spending is separated from other government spending.
- National income is the income received by all factors of production used in the generation of final output. It equals GDP minus the capital consumption allowance (depreciation) and a statistical discrepancy.
- Personal income reflects pretax income received by households. It equals national income plus transfers minus undistributed corporate profits, corporate income taxes, and indirect business taxes.
- Personal disposable income equals personal income minus personal taxes.
- Private saving must equal investment plus the fiscal and trade deficits. That is, $S = I + (G - T) + (X - M)$.
- Consumption spending is a function of disposable income. The marginal propensity to consume represents the fraction of an additional unit of disposable income that is spent.
- Investment spending depends on the average interest rate and the level of aggregate income. Government purchases and tax policy are often considered to be exogenous variables determined outside the macroeconomic model. Actual taxes collected depend on income and are, therefore, endogenous—that is, determined within the model.

- The IS curve reflects combinations of GDP and the real interest rate such that aggregate income/output equals planned expenditures. The LM curve reflects combinations of GDP and the interest rate such that demand and supply of real money balances are equal.
- Combining the IS and LM relationships yields the aggregate demand curve.
- Aggregate demand and aggregate supply determine the level of real GDP and the price level.
- The aggregate demand curve is the relationship between real output (GDP) demanded and the price level, holding underlying factors constant. Movements along the aggregate demand curve reflect the impact of price on demand.
- The aggregate demand curve is downward sloping because a rise in the price level reduces wealth, raises real interest rates, and raises the price of domestically produced goods versus foreign goods. The aggregate demand curve is drawn assuming a constant money supply.
- The aggregate demand curve will shift if there is a change in a factor (other than price) that affects aggregate demand. These factors include household wealth, consumer and business expectations, capacity utilization, monetary policy, fiscal policy, exchange rates, and foreign GDP.
- The aggregate supply curve is the relationship between the quantity of real GDP supplied and the price level, keeping all other factors constant. Movements along the supply curve reflect the impact of price on supply.
- The short-run aggregate supply curve is upward sloping because higher prices result in higher profits and induce businesses to produce more and laborers to work more. In the short run, some prices are sticky, implying that some prices do not adjust to changes in demand.
- In the long run, all prices are assumed to be flexible. The long-run aggregate supply curve is vertical because input costs adjust to changes in output prices, leaving the optimal level of output unchanged. The position of the curve is determined by the economy's level of potential GDP.
- The level of potential output, also called the full employment or natural level of output, is unobservable and difficult to measure precisely. This concept represents an efficient and unconstrained level of production at which companies have enough spare capacity to avoid bottlenecks and there is a balance between the pool of unemployed workers and the pool of job openings.
- The long-run aggregate supply curve will shift because of changes in labor supply, supply of physical and human capital, and productivity/technology.
- The short-run supply curve will shift because of changes in potential GDP, nominal wages, input prices, expectations about future prices, business taxes and subsidies, and the exchange rate.
- The business cycle and short-term fluctuations in GDP are caused by shifts in aggregate demand and aggregate supply.
- When the level of GDP in the economy is below potential GDP, such a recessionary situation exerts downward pressure on the aggregate price level.
- When the level of GDP is above potential GDP, such an overheated situation puts upward pressure on the aggregate price level.
- Stagflation, a combination of high inflation and weak economic growth, is caused by a decline in short-run aggregate supply.
- The sustainable rate of economic growth is measured by the rate of increase in the economy's productive capacity or potential GDP.
- Growth in real GDP measures how rapidly the total economy is expanding. Per capita GDP, defined as real GDP divided by population, reflects the standard of living in a country. Real GDP growth rates and levels of per capita GDP vary widely among countries.

- The sources of economic growth include the supply of labor, the supply of physical and human capital, raw materials, and technological knowledge.
- Output can be described in terms of a production function. For example, $Y = AF(L, K)$ where L is the quantity of labor, K is the capital stock, and A represents technological knowledge or total factor productivity. The function $F(\bullet)$ is assumed to exhibit constant returns to scale but diminishing marginal productivity for each input individually.
- Total factor productivity is a scale factor that reflects the portion of output growth that is not accounted for by changes in the capital and labor inputs. TFP is mainly a reflection of technological change.
- Based on a two-factor production function, Potential GDP growth = Growth in TFP + W_L (Growth in labor) + W_C (Growth in capital), where W_L and W_C ($= 1 - W_L$) are the shares of labor and capital in GDP.
- Diminishing marginal productivity implies that:
  - Increasing the supply of some input(s) relative to other inputs will lead to diminishing returns and cannot be the basis for sustainable growth. In particular, long-term sustainable growth cannot rely solely on capital deepening—that is, increasing the stock of capital relative to labor.
  - Given the relative scarcity and hence high productivity of capital in developing countries, the growth rates of developing countries should exceed those of developed countries.
- The labor supply is determined by population growth, the labor force participation rate, and net immigration. The capital stock in a country increases with investment. Correlation between long-run economic growth and the rate of investment is high.
- In addition to labor, capital, and technology, human capital—essentially, the quality of the labor force—and natural resources are important determinants of output and growth.
- Technological advances are discoveries that make it possible to produce more and higher-quality goods and services with the same resources or inputs. Technology is the main factor affecting economic growth in developed countries.
- The sustainable rate of growth in an economy is determined by the growth rate of the labor supply plus the growth rate of labor productivity.

PRACTICE PROBLEMS[1]

1. Which of the following statements is the *most* appropriate description of gross domestic product (GDP)?
   A. GDP is the total income earned by all households, firms, and the government whose value can be verified.
   B. GDP is the total amount spent on all final goods and services produced within the economy over a given time period.
   C. GDP is the total market value of resalable and final goods and services produced within the economy over a given time period.

---

[1]These practice problems were written by Ryan C. Fuhrmann, CFA (Westfield, Indiana, USA).

2. The component *least likely* to be included in a measurement of gross domestic product (GDP) is:
   A. the value of owner-occupied rent.
   B. the annual salary of a local police officer.
   C. environmental damage caused by production.

3. Which of the following conditions is *least likely* to increase a country's GDP?
   A. An increase in net exports
   B. Increased investment in capital goods
   C. Increased government transfer payments

4. Which of the following would be included in Canadian GDP for a given year? The market value of:
   A. wine grown in Canada by U.S. citizens.
   B. electronics made in Japan and sold in Canada.
   C. movies produced outside Canada by Canadian filmmakers.

5. Suppose a painting is created and sold in 2010 for £5,000. The expenses involved in producing the painting amounted to £2,000. According to the sum-of-value-added method of calculating GDP, the value added by the final step of creating the painting was:
   A. £2,000.
   B. £3,000.
   C. £5,000.

6. A GDP deflator less than 1 indicates that an economy has experienced:
   A. inflation.
   B. deflation.
   C. stagflation.

7. The *most* accurate description of nominal GDP is:
   A. a measure of total expenditures at current prices.
   B. the value of goods and services at constant prices.
   C. a measure to compare one nation's economy to another.

8. From the beginning to the ending years of a decade, the annual value of final goods and services for country X increased from €100 billion to €300 billion. Over that time period, the GDP deflator increased from 111 to 200. Over the decade, real GDP for country X increased by approximately:
   A. 50 percent.
   B. 67 percent.
   C. 200 percent.

9. If the GDP deflator values for 2008 and 2010 were 190 and 212.8, respectively, which of the following *best* describes the annual growth rate of the overall price level?
   A. 5.8 percent
   B. 6 percent
   C. 12 percent

10. The numerator of the GDP price deflator reflects:
    A. the value of base-year output at current prices.
    B. the value of current-year output at current prices.
    C. the value of current-year output at base-year prices.

11. Consider the following data for 2010 for a hypothetical country:

Account Name	Amount ($ trillions)
Consumption	15.0
Statistical discrepancy	0.5
Capital consumption allowance	1.5
Government spending	3.8
Imports	1.7
Gross private domestic investment	4.0
Exports	1.5

Based only on the data given, the gross domestic product and national income are respectively *closest* to:
    A. 21.1 and 20.6.
    B. 22.6 and 20.6.
    C. 22.8 and 20.8.

12. In calculating personal income for a given year, which of the following would *not* be subtracted from national income?
    A. Indirect business taxes
    B. Undistributed corporate profits
    C. Unincorporated business net income

13. Equality between aggregate expenditure and aggregate output implies that the government's fiscal deficit must equal:
    A. Private saving − Investment − Net exports.
    B. Private saving − Investment + Net exports.
    C. Investment − Private saving + Net exports.

14. Because of a sharp decline in real estate values, the household sector has increased the fraction of disposable income that it saves. If output and investment spending remain unchanged, which of the following is *most likely*?
    A. A decrease in the government deficit
    B. A decrease in net exports and increased capital inflow
    C. An increase in net exports and increased capital outflow

15. Which curve represents combinations of income and the real interest rate at which planned expenditure equals income?
    A. The IS curve
    B. The LM curve
    C. The aggregate demand curve

16. An increase in government spending would shift the:
    A. IS curve and the LM curve.
    B. IS curve and the aggregate demand curve.
    C. LM curve and the aggregate demand curve.

17. An increase in the nominal money supply would shift the:
    A. IS curve and the LM curve.
    B. IS curve and the aggregate demand curve.
    C. LM curve and the aggregate demand curve.

18. An increase in the price level would shift the:
    A. IS curve.
    B. LM curve.
    C. aggregate demand curve.

19. As the price level declines along the aggregate demand curve, the interest rate is *most likely* to:
    A. decline.
    B. increase.
    C. remain unchanged.

20. The full employment, or natural, level of output is *best* described as:
    A. the maximum level obtainable with existing resources.
    B. the level at which all available workers have jobs consistent with their skills.
    C. a level with a modest, stable pool of unemployed workers transitioning to new jobs.

21. Which of the following *best* describes the aggregate supply curve in the short run (e.g., one to two years)? The short run aggregate supply curve is:
    A. flat because output is more flexible than prices in the short run.
    B. vertical because wages and other input prices fully adjust to the price level.
    C. upward sloping because input prices do not fully adjust to the price level in the short run.

22. If wages were automatically adjusted for changes in the price level, the short-run aggregate supply curve would *most likely* be:
    A. more flat.
    B. steeper.
    C. unchanged.

23. The *least likely* cause of a decrease in aggregate demand is:
    A. higher taxes.
    B. a weak domestic currency.
    C. a fall in capacity utilization.

24. Which of the following is *most likely* to cause the long-run aggregate supply curve to shift to the left?
    A. Higher nominal wages
    B. A decline in productivity
    C. An increase in corporate taxes

25. Increased household wealth will *most likely* cause an increase in:
    A. household saving.
    B. investment expenditures.
    C. consumption expenditures.

26. The *most likely* outcome when both aggregate supply and aggregate demand increase is:
    A. a rise in inflation.
    B. higher employment.
    C. an increase in nominal GDP.

27. Which of the following is *least likely* to be caused by a shift in aggregate demand?
    A. Stagflation
    B. A recessionary gap
    C. An inflationary gap

28. Following a sharp increase in the price of energy, the overall price level is *most likely* to rise in the short run:
    A. and remain elevated indefinitely unless the central bank tightens.
    B. but be unchanged in the long run unless the money supply is increased.
    C. and continue to rise until all prices have increased by the same proportion.

29. Among developed economies, which of the following sources of economic growth is *most likely* to explain superior growth performance?
    A. Technology
    B. Capital stock
    C. Labor supply

30. Which of the following can be measured directly?
    A. Potential GDP
    B. Labor productivity
    C. Total factor productivity

31. The sustainable growth rate is *best* estimated as:
    A. the weighted average of capital and labor growth rates.
    B. growth in the labor force plus growth of labor productivity.
    C. growth in total factor productivity plus growth in the capital-to-labor ratio.

32. In the neoclassical or Solow growth model, an increase in total factor productivity reflects an increase in:
    A. returns to scale.
    B. output for given inputs.
    C. the sustainable growth rate.

The following information relates to Questions 33 and 34.

An economic forecasting firm has estimated the following equation from historical data based on the neoclassical growth model:

Potential output growth $= 1.5 + 0.72(\text{Growth of labor}) + 0.28(\text{Growth of capital})$

33. The intercept (1.5) in this equation is *best* interpreted as:
    A. the long-run sustainable growth rate.
    B. the growth rate of total factor productivity.
    C. above-trend historical growth that is unlikely to be sustained.

34. The coefficient on the growth rate of labor (0.72) in this equation is *best* interpreted as:
    A. the labor force participation rate.
    B. the marginal productivity of labor.
    C. the share of income earned by labor.

35. Convergence of incomes over time between emerging market countries and developed countries is *most likely* due to:
    A. total factor productivity.
    B. diminishing marginal productivity of capital.
    C. the exhaustion of nonrenewable resources.

CHAPTER 6

UNDERSTANDING BUSINESS CYCLES

LEARNING OUTCOMES

After completing this chapter, you will be able to do the following:

- Describe the business cycle and its phases.
- Explain the typical patterns of resource use fluctuation, housing sector activity, and external trade sector activity, as an economy moves through the business cycle.
- Describe theories of the business cycle.
- Describe types of unemployment and measures of unemployment.
- Explain inflation, hyperinflation, disinflation, and deflation.
- Explain the construction of indexes used to measure inflation.
- Compare inflation measures, including their uses and limitations.
- Distinguish between cost-push and demand-pull inflation.
- Describe economic indicators, including their uses and limitations.
- Identify the past, current, or expected future business cycle phase of an economy based on economic indicators.

SUMMARY OVERVIEW

- Business cycles are a fundamental feature of market economies, but their amplitude and length vary considerably.
- Business cycles have four phases: trough, expansion, peak, and contraction.
- Keynesian theories focus on fluctuations of aggregate demand (AD). If AD shifts left, Keynesians advocate government intervention to restore full employment and avoid a deflationary spiral. Monetarists argue that the timing of government policies is uncertain and it is generally better to let the economy find its new equilibrium unassisted, but to ensure that the money supply is kept growing at an even pace.
- New classical and real business cycle (RBC) theories also consider fluctuations of aggregate supply (AS). If AS shifts left because of an input price increase or right because of a price decrease or technical progress, the economy will gradually converge to its new equilibrium.

Government intervention is generally not necessary because it may exacerbate the fluctuation or delay the convergence to equilibrium. New Keynesians argue that frictions in the economy may prevent convergence, and government policies may be needed.

- The demand for factors of production may change in the short run as a result of changes in all components of GDP: consumption (e.g., households worry about the future, save more, and thus shift AD left); investment (e.g., companies expect customers to increase demand so they buy new equipment, thus shifting AD right; another example is that companies introduce new technologies, thus shifting long-term AS right); government (e.g., fiscal and monetary policies shift AD), and net exports (e.g., faster growth in other countries generates higher demand for the home country's products, thus shifting AD right, or higher prices of imported inputs shift AS left). Any shifts in AD and AS will affect the demand for the factors of production (capital and labor) that are used to produce the new level of GDP.

- Unemployment has different subcategories: frictional (people who are not working because they are between jobs); structural (people who are unemployed because they do not have the skills required by the openings or they reside far away from the jobs); discouraged workers, who are unemployed people who have given up looking for jobs because they do not believe they can find one (they are considered outside the labor force in unemployment statistics); and voluntarily unemployed people who do not wish to work, for example because they are in school, retired early, or are very rich (they are also considered outside the labor force in unemployment statistics).

- There are different types of inflation. Hyperinflation indicates a high (e.g., 100 percent annual) and increasing rate of inflation; deflation indicates a negative inflation rate (prices decrease); imported inflation is associated with increasing cost of inputs that come from abroad; demand inflation is caused by constraints in production that prevent companies from making as many goods as the market demands (it is sometimes called wartime inflation because goods tend to be rationed in times of war).

- Economic indicators are statistics on macroeconomic variables that help in understanding which stage of the business cycle an economy is at. Of particular importance are the leading indicators, which suggest where the economy is likely to be in the near future. No economic indicator is perfect, and many of these statistics are subject to periodic revisions.

- Price levels are affected by real factors and monetary factors. Real factors include aggregate supply (an increase in supply leads to lower prices) and aggregate demand (an increase in demand leads to higher prices). Monetary factors include the supply of money (more money circulating, if the economy is in equilibrium, will lead to higher prices) and the velocity of money (higher velocity, if the economy is in equilibrium, will lead to higher prices).

- Inflation is measured by many indexes. Consumer price indexes reflect the prices of a basket of goods and services that is typically purchased by a normal household. Producer price indexes measure the cost of a basket of raw materials, intermediate inputs, and finished products. GDP deflators measure the price of the basket of goods and services produced within an economy in a given year. Core indexes exclude volatile items, such as agricultural products and energy, whose prices tend to vary more than other goods.

PRACTICE PROBLEMS[1]

1. Business cycle analysis *most* commonly describes economic activity that is conducted through:
   A. state enterprises.
   B. agricultural co-ops.
   C. private corporations.

2. The characteristic business cycle patterns of trough, expansion, peak, and contraction are:
   A. periodic.
   B. recurrent.
   C. of similar duration.

3. During the contraction phase of a business cycle, it is *most likely* that:
   A. inflation indicators are stable.
   B. aggregate economic activity is decreasing.
   C. investor preference for government securities declines.

4. An economic peak is *most* closely associated with:
   A. accelerating inflation.
   B. stable unemployment.
   C. declining capital spending.

5. Based on typical labor utilization patterns across the business cycle, productivity (output per hours worked) is *most likely* to be highest:
   A. at the peak of a boom.
   B. into a maturing expansion.
   C. at the bottom of a recession.

6. In a recession, companies are *most likely* to adjust their stock of physical capital by:
   A. selling it at fire sale prices.
   B. not maintaining equipment.
   C. quickly canceling construction activity.

7. The inventory-to-sales ratio is *most likely* to be rising:
   A. as a contraction unfolds.
   B. partially into a recovery.
   C. near the top of an economic cycle.

8. The Austrian economic school attributes the primary cause of the business cycle to:
   A. misguided government intervention.
   B. the creative destruction of technological progress.
   C. sticky price and wage expectations that exaggerate trends.

---

[1]These practice problems were developed by Greg Gocek, CFA (Downers Grove, Illinois, USA).

9. Monetarists favor a limited role for the government because they argue that:
   A. government policies operate with a lag.
   B. firms take time to adjust to systemic shocks to the economy.
   C. resource use is efficient with marginal revenue and cost equal.

10. The discouraged worker category is defined to include people who:
    A. are overqualified for their jobs.
    B. could look for a job but choose not to.
    C. currently look for work without finding it.

11. The unemployment rate is considered a lagging indicator because:
    A. new job types must be defined to count their workers.
    B. multiworker households change jobs at a slower pace.
    C. businesses are slow to hire and fire due to related costs.

12. The factor for which it is *most* difficult to estimate its effect on the unemployment rate is:
    A. technological progress.
    B. the use of temporary workers.
    C. the nature of underemployment.

13. The category of persons who would be *most likely* to be harmed by an increase in the rate of inflation is:
    A. homeowners with fixed 30-year mortgages.
    B. retirees relying on a fixed annuity payment.
    C. workers employed under contracts with escalator clauses.

14. The term that describes when inflation declines but nonetheless remains at a positive level is:
    A. deflation.
    B. stagflation.
    C. disinflation.

15. Deflation is *most likely* to be associated with:
    A. a shortage of government revenue.
    B. substantial macroeconomic contraction.
    C. explicit monetary policy to combat inflation.

16. The *least likely* consequence of a period of hyperinflation is the:
    A. reduced velocity of money.
    B. increased supply of money.
    C. possibility of social unrest.

The following information relates to Questions 17 and 18.

Consumption Baskets and Prices over Two Months

Date	November 2010		December 2010	
Goods	Quantity	Price	Quantity	Price
Sugar	70 kg	€0.90/kg	120 kg	€1.00/kg
Cotton	60 kg	€0.60/kg	50 kg	€0.80/kg

17. Assuming the base period for 2010 consumption is November and the initial price index is set at 100, then the inflation rate after calculating the December price index as a Laspeyres index is *closest* to:
    A. 19.2 percent.
    B. 36.4 percent.
    C. 61.6 percent.

18. For the December consumption basket, the value of the Paasche index is *closest* to:
    A. 116.
    B. 148.
    C. 160.

19. The characteristic of national consumer price indexes that is *most* typically shared across major economies worldwide is:
    A. the geographic areas covered in their surveys.
    B. the weights they place on covered goods and services.
    C. their use in the determination of macroeconomic policy.

20. Of the following statements regarding the producer price index (PPI), which is the *least likely*?
    A. The PPI can influence the future CPI.
    B. The PPI category weights can vary more widely than analogous CPI terms.
    C. The PPI is used more frequently than CPI as a benchmark for adjusting labor contract payments.

21. The inflation rate *most likely* relied on to determine public economic policy is:
    A. core inflation.
    B. headline inflation.
    C. an index of food and energy prices.

22. What is the *most* important effect of labor productivity in a cost-push inflation scenario?
    A. Rising productivity indicates a strong economy and a bias toward inflation.
    B. The productivity level determines the economy's status relative to its natural rate of unemployment.
    C. As productivity growth proportionately exceeds wage increases, product price increases are less likely.

23. Which of the following statements is the *best* description of the characteristics of economic indicators?
    A. Leading indicators are important because they track the entire economy.
    B. Lagging indicators in measuring past conditions do not require revisions.
    C. A combination of leading and coincident indicators can offer effective forecasts.

24. When the spread between 10-year U.S. Treasury yields and the federal funds rate narrows and at the same time the prime rate stays unchanged, this mix of indicators *most likely* forecasts future economic:
    A. growth.
    B. decline.
    C. stability.

25. If relative to prior values of their respective indicators, the inventory-to-sales ratio has risen, unit labor cost is stable, and real personal income has decreased, it is *most likely* that a peak in the business cycle:
    A. has occurred.
    B. is just about to occur.
    C. will occur sometime in the future.

CHAPTER 7

MONETARY AND FISCAL POLICY

LEARNING OUTCOMES

After completing this chapter, you will be able to do the following:

- Compare monetary policy and fiscal policy.
- Describe functions and definitions of money.
- Explain the money creation process.
- Describe theories of the demand for and supply of money.
- Describe the Fisher effect.
- Describe the roles and objectives of central banks.
- Contrast the costs of expected and unexpected inflation.
- Describe the implementation of monetary policy.
- Describe the qualities of effective central banks.
- Explain the relationships between monetary policy and economic growth, inflation, interest, and exchange rates.
- Contrast the use of inflation, interest rate, and exchange rate targeting by central banks.
- Determine whether a monetary policy is expansionary or contractionary.
- Describe the limitations of monetary policy.
- Describe the roles and objectives of fiscal policy.
- Describe the tools of fiscal policy, including their advantages and disadvantages.
- Describe the arguments for and against being concerned with the size of a fiscal deficit relative to gross domestic product (GDP).
- Explain the implementation of fiscal policy and the difficulties of implementation.
- Determine whether a fiscal policy is expansionary or contractionary.
- Explain the interaction of monetary policy and fiscal policy.

SUMMARY OVERVIEW

- Governments can influence the performance of their economies by using combinations of monetary and fiscal policy. Monetary policy refers to central bank activities that are directed toward influencing the quantity of money and credit in an economy. By contrast, fiscal policy refers to the government's decisions about taxation and spending. The two sets of policies affect the economy via different mechanisms.

- Money fulfills three important functions: It acts as a medium of exchange, provides individuals with a way of storing wealth, and provides society with a convenient unit of account. Via the process of fractional reserve banking, the banking system can create money.

- The amount of wealth that the citizens of an economy choose to hold in the form of money—as opposed to, for example, bonds or equities—is known as the demand for money. There are three basic motives for holding money: transactions-related, precautionary, and speculative.

- The addition of one unit of additional reserves to a fractional reserve banking system can support an expansion of the money supply by an amount equal to the money multiplier, defined as 1/reserve requirement (stated as a decimal).

- The nominal rate of interest is comprised of three components: a real required rate of return, a component to compensate lenders for future inflation, and a risk premium to compensate lenders for uncertainty (e.g., about the future rate of inflation).

- Central banks take on multiple roles in modern economies. They are usually the monopoly supplier of their currency, the lender of last resort to the banking sector, the government's bank, and the banks' bank, and they often supervise banks. Although they may express their objectives in different ways, the overarching objective of most central banks is price stability.

- For a central bank to be able to implement monetary policy objectively, it should have a degree of independence from government, be credible, and be transparent in its goals and objectives.

- The ultimate challenge for central banks as they try to manipulate the supply of money to influence the economy is that they cannot control the amount of money that households and corporations put in banks on deposit, nor can they easily control the willingness of banks to create money by expanding credit. Taken together, this also means that they cannot always control the money supply. Therefore, there are definite limits to the power of monetary policy.

- The concept of money neutrality is usually interpreted as meaning that money cannot influence the real economy in the long run. However, by the setting of its policy rate, a central bank hopes to influence the real economy via the policy rate's impact on other market interest rates, asset prices, the exchange rate, and the expectations of economic agents.

- Inflation targeting is the most common monetary policy—although exchange rate targeting is also used, particularly in developing economies. Quantitative easing attempts to spur aggregate demand by drastically increasing the money supply.

- Fiscal policy involves the use of government spending and revenue raising (taxation) to impact a number of aspects of the economy: the overall level of aggregate demand in an economy and hence the level of economic activity, the distribution of income and wealth among different segments of the population, and hence ultimately the allocation of resources among different sectors and economic agents.

- The tools that governments use in implementing fiscal policy are related to the way in which they raise revenue and the different forms of expenditure. Governments usually raise money via a combination of direct and indirect taxes. Government expenditure can be current on goods and services or can take the form of capital expenditure—for example, on infrastructure projects.

- As economic growth weakens or when it is in recession, a government can enact an expansionary fiscal policy—for example, by raising expenditures without an offsetting increase in taxation. Conversely, by reducing expenditures and maintaining tax revenues, a contractionary policy might reduce economic activity. Fiscal policy can therefore play an important role in stabilizing an economy.

• Although both fiscal and monetary policy can alter aggregate demand, they work through different channels; the policies are therefore not interchangeable, and they conceivably can work against one another unless the government and central bank coordinate their objectives.

PRACTICE PROBLEMS[1]

1. As the reserve requirement increases, the money multiplier:
   A. increases.
   B. decreases.
   C. remains the same.

2. Which is the *most* accurate statement regarding the demand for money?
   A. Precautionary money demand is directly related to GDP.
   B. Transactions money demand is inversely related to returns on bonds.
   C. Speculative demand is inversely related to the perceived risk of other assets.

3. The following exhibit shows the supply and demand for money:

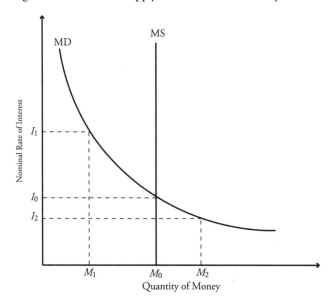

There is an excess supply of money when the nominal rate of interest is:
A. I_0.
B. I_1.
C. I_2.

---

[1]These practice problems were developed by Karen O'Connor Rubsam, CFA (Fountain Hills, Arizona, USA).

4. According to the theory of money neutrality, money supply growth does *not* affect variables such as real output and employment in:
   A. the long run.
   B. the short run.
   C. the long run and the short run.

5. Which of the following *best* describes a fundamental assumption when monetary policy is used to influence the economy?
   A. Financial markets are efficient.
   B. Money is not neutral in the short run.
   C. Official rates do not affect exchange rates.

6. Monetarists are *most likely* to believe that:
   A. there is a causal relationship running from inflation to money.
   B. inflation can be affected by changing the money supply growth rate.
   C. rapid financial innovation in the market increases the effectiveness of monetary policy.

7. The proposition that the real interest rate is relatively stable is *most* closely associated with:
   A. the Fisher effect.
   B. money neutrality.
   C. the quantity theory of money.

8. Which of the following equations is a consequence of the Fisher effect?
   A. Nominal interest rate = Real interest rate + Expected rate of inflation
   B. Real interest rate = Nominal interest rate + Expected rate of inflation
   C. Nominal interest rate = Real interest rate + Market risk premium

9. Central banks would typically be *most* concerned with costs of:
   A. low levels of inflation that are anticipated.
   B. moderate levels of inflation that are anticipated.
   C. moderate levels of inflation that are not anticipated.

10. Monetary policy is *least likely* to include:
    A. setting an inflation rate target.
    B. changing an official interest rate.
    C. enacting a transfer payment program.

11. Which role is a central bank *least likely* to assume?
    A. Lender of last resort
    B. Sole supervisor of banks
    C. Supplier of the currency

12. Which is the *most* accurate statement regarding central banks and monetary policy?
    A. Central bank activities are typically intended to maintain price stability.
    B. Monetary policies work through the economy via four independent channels.
    C. Commercial and interbank interest rates move inversely to official interest rates.

13. When a central bank announces a decrease in its official policy rate, the desired impact is an increase in:
    A. investment.
    B. interbank borrowing rates.
    C. the national currency's value in exchange for other currencies.

14. Which action is a central bank *least likely* to take if it wants to encourage businesses and households to borrow for investment and consumption purposes?
    A. Sell long-dated government securities.
    B. Purchase long-dated government Treasuries.
    C. Purchase mortgage bonds or other securities.

15. A central bank that decides the desired levels of interest rates and inflation and the horizon over which the inflation objective is to be achieved is *most* accurately described as being:
    A. target independent and operationally independent.
    B. target independent but not operationally independent.
    C. operationally independent but not target independent.

16. A country that maintains a target exchange rate is *most likely* to have which outcome when its inflation rate rises above the level of the inflation rate in the target country?
    A. An increase in short-term interest rates
    B. An increase in the domestic money supply
    C. An increase in its foreign currency reserves

17. A central bank's repeated open market purchases of government bonds:
    A. decrease the money supply.
    B. are prohibited in most countries.
    C. are consistent with an expansionary monetary policy.

18. In theory, setting the policy rate equal to the neutral interest rate should promote:
    A. stable inflation.
    B. a balanced budget.
    C. greater employment.

19. A prolonged period of an official interest rate of zero without an increase in economic growth *most likely* suggests that:
    A. quantitative easing must be limited to be successful.
    B. there may be limits to the effectiveness of monetary policy.
    C. targeting reserve levels is more important than targeting interest rates.

20. Raising the reserve requirement is *most likely* an example of which type of monetary policy?
    A. Neutral
    B. Expansionary
    C. Contractionary

21. Which of the following is a limitation on the ability of central banks to stimulate growth in periods of deflation?
    A. Ricardian equivalence
    B. The interaction of monetary and fiscal policy
    C. The fact that interest rates have a minimum value (zero percent)

22. The *least likely* limitation to the effectiveness of monetary policy is that central banks cannot:
    A. accurately determine the neutral rate of interest.
    B. regulate the willingness of financial institutions to lend.
    C. control amounts that economic agents deposit into banks.

23. Which of the following is the *most likely* example of a tool of fiscal policy?
    A. Public financing of a power plant
    B. Regulation of the payment system
    C. Central bank's purchase of government bonds

24. The *least likely* goal of a government's fiscal policy is to:
    A. redistribute income and wealth.
    B. influence aggregate national output.
    C. ensure the stability of the purchasing power of its currency.

25. Given an independent central bank, monetary policy actions are *more likely* than fiscal policy actions to be:
    A. implementable quickly.
    B. effective when a specific group is targeted.
    C. effective when combating a deflationary economy.

26. Which statement regarding fiscal policy is *most* accurate?
    A. To raise business capital spending, personal income taxes should be reduced.
    B. Cyclically adjusted budget deficits are appropriate indicators of fiscal policy.
    C. An increase in the budget surplus is associated with expansionary fiscal policy.

27. The *least likely* explanation for why fiscal policy cannot stabilize aggregate demand completely is that:
    A. private-sector behavior changes over time.
    B. policy changes are implemented very quickly.
    C. fiscal policy focuses more on inflation than on unemployment.

28. Which of the following *best* represents a contractionary fiscal policy?
    A. Public spending on a high-speed railway
    B. A temporary suspension of payroll taxes
    C. A freeze in discretionary government spending

29. A pay-as-you-go rule, which requires that any tax cut or increase in entitlement spending be offset by an increase in other taxes or reduction in other entitlement spending, is an example of which fiscal policy stance?
    A. Neutral
    B. Expansionary
    C. Contractionary

30. Quantitative easing, the purchase of government or private securities by the central banks from individuals and institutions, is an example of which monetary policy stance?
    A. Neutral
    B. Expansionary
    C. Contractionary

31. The *most likely* argument against high national debt levels is that:
    A. the debt is owed internally to fellow citizens.
    B. they create disincentives for economic activity.
    C. they may finance investment in physical and human capital.

32. Which statement regarding fiscal deficits is *most* accurate?
    A. Higher government spending may lead to higher interest rates and lower private-sector investing.
    B. Central bank actions that grow the money supply to address deflationary conditions decrease fiscal deficits.
    C. According to the Ricardian equivalence, deficits have a multiplicative effect on consumer spending.

33. Which policy alternative is *most likely* to be effective for growing both the public and private sectors?
    A. Easy fiscal policy/easy monetary policy
    B. Easy fiscal policy/tight monetary policy
    C. Tight fiscal policy/tight monetary policy

CHAPTER 8

INTERNATIONAL TRADE AND CAPITAL FLOWS

LEARNING OUTCOMES

After completing this chapter, you will be able to do the following:

- Compare gross domestic product and gross national product.
- Describe the benefits and costs of international trade.
- Distinguish between comparative advantage and absolute advantage.
- Explain the Ricardian and Heckscher–Ohlin models of trade and the source(s) of comparative advantage in each model.
- Compare types of trade and capital restrictions and their economic implications.
- Explain motivations for and advantages of trading blocs, common markets, and economic unions.
- Describe the balance of payments accounts, including their components.
- Explain how decisions by consumers, firms, and governments affect the balance of payments.
- Describe functions and objectives of the international organizations that facilitate trade, including the World Bank, the International Monetary Fund, and the World Trade Organization.

SUMMARY OVERVIEW

- The benefits of trade include:
  - Gains from exchange and specialization.
  - Gains from economies of scale as companies add new markets for their products.
  - Greater variety of products available to households and firms.
  - Increased competition and more efficient allocation of resources.
- A country has an absolute advantage in producing a good (or service) if it is able to produce that good at a lower absolute cost or use fewer resources in its production than its trading partner. A country has a comparative advantage in producing a good if its *opportunity cost* of producing that good is less than that of its trading partner.

- Even if a country does not have an absolute advantage in the production of any good, it can gain from trade by producing and exporting the good(s) in which it has a comparative advantage and importing good(s) in which it has a comparative disadvantage.
- In the Ricardian model of trade, comparative advantage and the pattern of trade are determined by differences in technology between countries. In the Heckscher–Ohlin model of trade, comparative advantage and the pattern of trade are determined by differences in factor endowments between countries. In reality, technology and factor endowments are complementary, not mutually exclusive, determinants of trade patterns.
- Trade barriers prevent the free flow of goods and services among countries. Governments impose trade barriers for various reasons, including to promote specific developmental objectives, to counteract certain imperfections in the functioning of markets, or to respond to problems facing their economies.
- For purposes of international trade policy and analysis, a small country is defined as one that cannot affect the world price of traded goods. A large country's production and/or consumption decisions do alter the relative prices of trade goods.
- In a small country, trade barriers generate a net welfare loss arising from distortion of production and consumption decisions and the associated inefficient allocation of resources.
- Trade barriers can generate a net welfare gain in a large country if the gain from improving its terms of trade (higher export prices and lower import prices) more than offsets the loss from the distortion of resource allocations. However, the large country can gain only if it imposes an even larger welfare loss on its trading partner(s).
- An import tariff and an import quota have the same effect on price, production, and trade. With a quota, however, some or all of the revenue that would be raised by the equivalent tariff is instead captured by foreign producers (or the foreign government) as quota rents. Thus, the welfare loss suffered by the importing country is generally greater with a quota.
- A voluntary export restraint is imposed by the exporting country. It has the same impact on the importing country as an import quota from which foreigners capture all of the quota rents.
- An export subsidy encourages firms to export their product rather than sell it in the domestic market. The distortion of production, consumption, and trade decisions generates a welfare loss. The welfare loss is greater for a large country because increased production, and export, of the subsidized product reduces its global price—that is, worsens the country's terms of trade.
- Capital restrictions are defined as controls placed on foreigners' ability to own domestic assets and/or domestic residents' ability to own foreign assets. In contrast to trade restrictions, which limit the openness of goods markets, capital restrictions limit the openness of financial markets.
- A regional trading bloc is a group of countries that have signed an agreement to reduce and progressively eliminate barriers to trade and movement of factors of production among the members of the bloc.
  - The bloc may or may not have common trade barriers against those countries that are not members of the bloc. In a free trade area all barriers to the flow of goods and services among members are eliminated, but each country maintains its own polices against nonmembers.
  - A customs union extends the FTA by not only allowing free movement of goods and services among members but also creating a common trade policy against nonmembers.
  - A common market incorporates all aspects of a customs union and extends it by allowing free movement of factors of production among members.

- An economic union incorporates all aspects of a common market and requires common economic institutions and coordination of economic policies among members.
  - Members of a monetary union adopt a common currency.
- From an investment perspective, it is important to understand the complex and dynamic nature of trading relationships because they can help identify potential profitable investment opportunities as well as provide some advance warning signals regarding when to disinvest in a market or industry.
- The major components of the balance of payments are:
  - The current account balance, which largely reflects trade in goods and services.
  - The capital account balance, which mainly consists of capital transfers and net sales of nonproduced, nonfinancial assets.
  - The financial account, which measures net capital flows based on sales and purchases of domestic and foreign financial assets.
- Decisions by consumers, firms, and governments influence the balance of payments.
  - Low private savings and/or high investment tend to produce a current account deficit that must be financed by net capital imports; high private savings and/or low investment, however, produce a current account surplus, balanced by net capital exports.
  - All else being the same, a government deficit produces a current account deficit and a government surplus leads to a current account surplus.
  - All else being the same, a sustained current account deficit contributes to a rise in the risk premium for financial assets of the deficit country. Current account surplus countries tend to enjoy lower risk premiums than current account deficit countries.
- Created after World War II, the International Monetary Fund, the World Bank, and the World Trade Organization are the three major international organizations that provide necessary stability to the international monetary system and facilitate international trade and development.
  - The IMF's mission is to ensure the stability of the international monetary system, the system of exchange rates and international payments that enables countries to buy goods and services from each other. The IMF helps to keep country-specific market risk and global systemic risk under control.
  - The World Bank helps to create the basic economic infrastructure essential for creation and maintenance of domestic financial markets and a well-functioning financial industry in developing countries.
  - The World Trade Organization's mission is to foster free trade by providing a major institutional and regulatory framework of global trade rules; without this framework it would be hard to conceive of today's global multinational corporations.

PRACTICE PROBLEMS[1]

1. Which of the following statements *best* describes the benefits of international trade?
   A. Countries gain from exchange and specialization.
   B. Countries receive lower prices for their exports and pay higher prices for imports.
   C. Absolute advantage is required for a country to benefit from trade in the long term.

---

[1]These practice problems were developed by Drew H. Boecher, CFA (Dedham, Massachusetts, USA).

2. Which of the following statements *best* describes the costs of international trade?
   A. Countries without an absolute advantage in producing a good cannot benefit significantly from international trade.
   B. Resources may need to be allocated into or out of an industry, and less efficient companies may be forced to exit an industry, which in turn may lead to higher unemployment.
   C. Loss of manufacturing jobs in developed countries as a result of import competition means that developed countries benefit far less than developing countries from trade.

3. Suppose the cost of producing tea relative to copper is lower in Tealand than in Copperland. With trade, the copper industry in Copperland would *most likely*:
   A. expand.
   B. contract.
   C. remain stable.

4. A country has a comparative advantage in producing a good if:
   A. it is able to produce the good at a lower cost than its trading partner.
   B. its opportunity cost of producing the good is less than that of its trading partner.
   C. its opportunity cost of producing the good is more than that of its trading partner.

5. Suppose Mexico exports vegetables to Brazil and imports flashlights used for mining from Brazil. The output per worker per day in each country is as follows:

	Flashlights	Vegetables
Mexico	20	60
Brazil	40	80

   Which country has a comparative advantage in the production of vegetables, and what is the *most* relevant opportunity cost?
   A. Brazil: 2 vegetables per flashlight
   B. Mexico: 1.5 vegetables per flashlight
   C. Mexico: ⅓ flashlight per vegetable

6. Suppose three countries produce rulers and pencils with output per worker per day in each country as follows:

	Rulers	Pencils
Mexico	20	40
Brazil	30	90
China	40	160

   Which country has the greatest comparative advantage in the production of rulers?
   A. China
   B. Brazil
   C. Mexico

7. In the Ricardian trade model, comparative advantage is determined by:
   A. technology.
   B. the capital-to-labor ratio.
   C. the level of labor productivity.

8. In the Ricardian trade model, a country captures more of the gains from trade if:
   A. it produces all products while its trade partner specializes in one good.
   B. the terms of trade are closer to its autarkic prices than to its partner's autarkic prices.
   C. the terms of trade are closer to its partner's autarkic prices than to its autarkic prices.

9. Germany has much more capital per worker than Portugal. In autarky each country produces and consumes both machine tools and wine. Production of machine tools is relatively capital intensive whereas winemaking is labor intensive. According to the Heckscher–Ohlin model, when trade opens:
   A. Germany should export machine tools and Portugal should export wine.
   B. Germany should export wine and Portugal should export machine tools.
   C. Germany should produce only machine tools and Portugal should produce only wine.

10. According to the Heckscher–Ohlin model, when trade opens:
    A. the scarce factor gains relative to the abundant factor in each country.
    B. the abundant factor gains relative to the scarce factor in each country.
    C. income is redistributed between countries but not within each country.

11. Which type of trade restriction would *most likely* increase domestic government revenue?
    A. A tariff
    B. An import quota
    C. An export subsidy

12. Which of the following trade restrictions is *most likely* to result in the greatest welfare loss for the importing country?
    A. A tariff
    B. An import quota
    C. A voluntary export restraint

13. A large country can:
    A. benefit by imposing a tariff.
    B. benefit with an export subsidy.
    C. not benefit from any trade restriction.

14. If Brazil and South Africa have free trade with each other, a common trade policy against all other countries, but no free movement of factors of production between them, then Brazil and South Africa are part of a:
    A. customs union.
    B. common market.
    C. free trade area (FTA).

15. Which of the following factors *best* explains why regional trading agreements are more popular than larger multilateral trade agreements?
    A. Minimal displacement costs
    B. Trade diversions that benefit members
    C. Quicker and easier policy coordination

16. The sale of mineral rights would be captured in which of the following balance of payments components?
    A. Capital account
    B. Current account
    C. Financial account

17. Patent fees and legal services are recorded in which of the following balance of payments components?
    A. Capital account
    B. Current account
    C. Financial account

18. During the most recent quarter, a steel company in South Korea had the following transactions:

    • The company bought iron ore from Australia for AUD50 million.
    • It sold finished steel to the United States for USD65 million.
    • It borrowed AUD50 million from a bank in Sydney.
    • It received a USD10 million dividend from a U.S. subsidiary.
    • It paid KRW550 million to a South Korean shipping company.

    Which of the following would be reflected in South Korea's current account balance for the quarter?
    A. The loan
    B. The shipping
    C. The dividend

19. Which of the following *most likely* contributes to a current account deficit?
    A. High taxes
    B. Low private savings
    C. Low private investment

20. Which of the following chronic deficit conditions is *least* alarming to the deficit country's creditors?
    A. High consumption
    B. High private investment
    C. High government spending

21. Which of the following international trade organizations regulates cross-border exchange among nations on a global scale?
    A. World Bank Group (World Bank)
    B. World Trade Organization (WTO)
    C. International Monetary Fund (IMF)

22. Which of the following international trade organizations has a mission to help developing countries fight poverty and enhance environmentally sound economic growth?
    A. World Bank Group (World Bank)
    B. World Trade Organization (WTO)
    C. International Monetary Fund (IMF)

23. Which of the following organizations helps to keep global systemic risk under control by preventing contagion in scenarios such as the 2010 Greek sovereign debt crisis?
    A. World Bank Group (World Bank)
    B. World Trade Organization (WTO)
    C. International Monetary Fund (IMF)

24. Which of the following international trade bodies was the only multilateral body governing international trade from 1948 to 1995?
    A. World Trade Organization (WTO)
    B. International Trade Organization (ITO)
    C. General Agreement on Tariffs and Trade (GATT)

CHAPTER 9

CURRENCY EXCHANGE RATES

LEARNING OUTCOMES

After completing this chapter, you will be able to do the following:

- Define an exchange rate, and distinguish between nominal and real exchange rates and spot and forward exchange rates.
- Describe functions of and participants in the foreign exchange market.
- Calculate and interpret the percentage change in a currency relative to another currency.
- Calculate and interpret currency cross-rates.
- Convert a forward quotation expressed on a points basis or in percentage terms into an outright forward quotation.
- Explain the arbitrage relationships between spot rates, forward rates, and interest rates.
- Calculate and interpret a forward discount or premium.
- Calculate and interpret the forward rate consistent with the spot rate and the interest rate in each currency.
- Describe exchange rate regimes.
- Explain the impact of exchange rates on countries' international trade and capital flows.

SUMMARY OVERVIEW

- Measured by average daily turnover, the foreign exchange market is by far the largest financial market in the world. It has important effects, either directly or indirectly, on the pricing and flows in all other financial markets.
- There is a wide diversity of global FX market participants that have a wide variety of motives for entering into foreign exchange transactions.
- Individual currencies are usually referred to by standardized three-character codes. These currency codes can also be used to define exchange rates (the price of one currency in terms of another). There are a variety of exchange rate quoting conventions commonly used.
- A direct currency quote takes the domestic currency as the price currency and the foreign currency as the base currency (i.e., $S_{d/f}$). An indirect quote uses the domestic currency as the base currency (i.e., $S_{f/d}$). To convert between direct and indirect quotes, the inverse

(reciprocal) is used. Professional FX markets use standardized conventions for how the exchange rate for specific currency pairs will be quoted.

- Currencies trade in foreign exchange markets based on nominal exchange rates. An increase in the exchange rate, quoted in indirect terms, means that the domestic currency is appreciating versus the foreign currency, and a decrease in the exchange rate means the domestic currency is depreciating.

- The real exchange rate, defined as the nominal exchange rate multiplied by the ratio of price levels, measures the relative purchasing power of the currencies. An increase in the real exchange rate ($R_{d/f}$) implies a reduction in the relative purchasing power of the domestic currency.

- Given exchange rates for two currency pairs—A/B and A/C—we can compute the cross-rate (B/C) between currencies B and C. Depending on how the rates are quoted, this may require inversion of one of the quoted rates.

- Spot exchange rates are for immediate settlement (typically, $T + 2$), while forward exchange rates are for settlement at agreed-upon future dates. Forward rates can be used to manage foreign exchange risk exposures or can be combined with spot transactions to create FX swaps.

- The spot exchange rate, the forward exchange rate, and the domestic and foreign interest rates must jointly satisfy an arbitrage relationship that equates the investment return on two alternative but equivalent investments. Given the spot exchange rate and the foreign and domestic interest rates, the forward exchange rate must take the value that prevents riskless arbitrage.

- Forward rates are typically quoted in terms of forward (or swap) points. The swap points are added to the spot exchange rate in order to calculate the forward rate. Occasionally, forward rates are presented in terms of percentages relative to the spot rate.

- The base currency is said to be trading at a forward premium if the forward rate is above the spot rate (forward points are positive). Conversely, the base currency is said to be trading at a forward discount if the forward rate is below the spot rate (forward points are negative).

- The currency with the higher interest rate will trade at a forward discount, and the currency with the lower interest rate will trade at a forward premium.

- Swap points are proportional to the spot exchange rate and to the interest rate differential and approximately proportional to the term of the forward contract.

- Empirical studies suggest that forward exchange rates may be unbiased predictors of future spot rates, but the margin of error on such forecasts is too large for them to be used in practice as a guide to managing exchange rate exposures. FX markets are too complex and too intertwined with other global financial markets to be adequately characterized by a single variable, such as the interest rate differential.

- Virtually every exchange rate is managed to some degree by central banks. The policy framework that each central bank adopts is called an exchange rate regime. These regimes range from using another country's currency (dollarization) to letting the market determine the exchange rate (independent float). In practice, most regimes fall in between these extremes. The type of exchange rate regime used varies widely among countries and over time.

- An ideal currency regime would have three properties: (1) the exchange rate between any two currencies would be credibly fixed; (2) all currencies would be fully convertible; and (3) each country would be able to undertake fully independent monetary policy in pursuit of domestic objectives, such as growth and inflation targets. However, these conditions are inconsistent. In particular, a fixed exchange rate and unfettered capital flows severely limit a country's ability to undertake independent monetary policy. Hence, there cannot be an ideal currency regime.

- The IMF identifies the following types of regimes: dollarization, monetary union, currency board, fixed parity, target zone, crawling peg, crawling band, managed float, and independent float. Most major currencies traded in FX markets are freely floating, albeit subject to occasional central bank intervention.
- A trade surplus must be matched by a corresponding deficit in the capital account, and a trade deficit must be matched by a capital account surplus. Any factor that affects the trade balance must have an equal and opposite impact on the capital account, and vice versa.
- A trade surplus reflects an excess of domestic saving (including the government fiscal balance) over investment spending. A trade deficit indicates that the country invests more than it saves and must finance the excess by borrowing from foreigners or selling assets to foreigners.
- The impact of the exchange rate on trade and capital flows can be analyzed from two perspectives. The elasticities approach focuses on the effect of changing the relative prices of domestic and foreign goods. This approach highlights changes in the composition of spending. The absorption approach focuses on the impact of exchange rates on aggregate expenditure/saving decisions.
- The elasticities approach leads to the Marshall–Lerner condition, which describes combinations of export and import demand elasticities such that depreciation of the domestic currency will move the trade balance toward surplus, and domestic currency appreciation will move the trade balance toward deficit.
- The idea underlying the Marshall–Lerner condition is that demand for imports and exports must be sufficiently price sensitive that an increase in the relative prices of imports increases the difference between export receipts and import expenditures.
- In order to move the trade balance toward surplus, a change in the exchange rate must decrease domestic expenditure (also called absorption) relative to income; to move the trade balance toward deficit, a change in the exchange rate must increase domestic expenditure. Equivalently, it must increase (or decrease) domestic saving relative to domestic investment.
- If there is excess capacity in the economy, then currency depreciation can increase output/income by switching demand toward domestically produced goods and services. Because some of the additional income will be saved, income rises relative to expenditure and the trade balance improves.
- If the economy is at full employment, then currency depreciation must reduce domestic expenditure in order to improve the trade balance. The main mechanism is a wealth effect: A weaker currency reduces the purchasing power of domestic-currency-denominated assets (including the present value of current and future earned income), and households respond by reducing expenditure and increasing saving.

PRACTICE PROBLEMS[1]

1. An exchange rate:
   A. is most commonly quoted in real terms.
   B. is the price of one currency in terms of another.
   C. between two currencies ensures that they are fully convertible.

---

[1]These practice problems were developed by Ryan Fuhrmann, CFA (Westfield, Indiana, USA).

2. A decrease in the real exchange rate (quoted in terms of domestic currency per unit of foreign currency) is *most likely* to be associated with an increase in which of the following?
   A. Foreign price level
   B. Domestic price level
   C. Nominal exchange rate

3. In order to minimize the foreign exchange exposure on a euro-denominated receivable due from a German company in 100 days, a British company would *most likely* initiate a:
   A. spot transaction.
   B. forward contract.
   C. real exchange rate contract.

4. Which of the following counterparties is *most likely* to be considered a sell-side foreign exchange market participant?
   A. A large corporation that borrows in foreign currencies
   B. A sovereign wealth fund that influences cross-border capital flows
   C. A multinational bank that trades foreign exchange with its diverse client base

5. What will be the effect on a direct exchange rate quote if the domestic currency appreciates?
   A. Increase
   B. Decrease
   C. No change

6. An executive from Switzerland checked into a hotel room in Spain and was told by the hotel manager that 1 EUR will buy 1.2983 CHF. From the executive's perspective, an indirect exchange rate quote would be:
   A. 0.7702 EUR per CHF.
   B. 0.7702 CHF per EUR.
   C. 1.2983 EUR per CHF.

7. Over the past month, the Swiss franc (CHF) has depreciated 12 percent against pound sterling (GBP). How much has the pound sterling appreciated against the Swiss franc?
   A. Exactly 12 percent
   B. Less than 12 percent
   C. More than 12 percent

8. An exchange rate between two currencies has increased to 1.4500. If the base currency has appreciated by 8 percent against the price currency, the initial exchange rate between the two currencies was *closest* to:
   A. 1.3340.
   B. 1.3426.
   C. 1.5660.

The following information relates to Questions 9 and 10.

A dealer provides the following quotes:

Ratio	Spot Rate
CNY/HKD	0.8422
CNY/ZAR	0.9149
CNY/SEK	1.0218

9. The spot ZAR/HKD cross-rate is *closest* to:
   A. 0.9205.
   B. 1.0864.
   C. 1.2978.

10. Another dealer is quoting the ZAR/SEK cross-rate at 1.1210. The arbitrage profit that can be earned is *closest* to:
    A. ZAR3,671 per million SEK traded.
    B. SEK4,200 per million ZAR traded.
    C. ZAR4,200 per million SEK traded.

11. A BRL/MXN spot rate is listed by a dealer at 0.1378. The six-month forward rate is 0.14193. The six-month forward points are *closest* to:
    A. −41.3.
    B. +41.3.
    C. +299.7.

12. A three-month forward exchange rate in CAD/USD is listed by a dealer at 1.0123. The dealer also quotes three-month forward points as a percentage at 6.8 percent. The CAD/USD spot rate is *closest* to:
    A. 0.9478.
    B. 1.0550.
    C. 1.0862.

13. If the base currency in a forward exchange rate quote is trading at a forward discount, which of the following statements is *most* accurate?
    A. The forward points will be positive.
    B. The forward percentage will be negative.
    C. The base currency is expected to appreciate versus the price currency.

14. A forward premium indicates:
    A. an expected increase in demand for the base currency.
    B. that the interest rate is higher in the base currency than in the price currency.
    C. that the interest rate is higher in the price currency than in the base currency.

15. The JPY/AUD spot exchange rate is 82.42, the JPY interest rate is 0.15 percent, and the AUD interest rate is 4.95 percent. If the interest rates are quoted on the basis of a 360-day year, the 90-day forward points in JPY/AUD would be *closest* to:
    A. −377.0.
    B. −97.7.
    C. 98.9.

16. Which of the following is *not* a condition of an ideal currency regime?
    A. Fully convertible currencies
    B. Fully independent monetary policy
    C. Independently floating exchange rates

17. In practice, both a fixed parity regime and a target zone regime allow the exchange rate to float within a band around the parity level. The *most likely* rationale for the band is that the band allows the monetary authority to:
    A. be less active in the currency market.
    B. earn a spread on its currency transactions.
    C. exercise more discretion in monetary policy.

18. A fixed exchange rate regime in which the monetary authority is legally required to hold foreign exchange reserves backing 100 percent of its domestic currency issuance is best described as:
    A. dollarization.
    B. a currency board.
    C. a monetary union.

19. A country with a trade deficit will *most likely*:
    A. have an offsetting capital account surplus.
    B. save enough to fund its investment spending.
    C. buy assets from foreigners to fund the imbalance.

20. A large industrialized country has recently devalued its currency in an attempt to correct a persistent trade deficit. Which of the following domestic industries is *most likely* to benefit from the devaluation?
    A. Luxury cars
    B. Branded prescription drugs
    C. Restaurants and live entertainment venues

21. A country with a persistent trade surplus is being pressured to let its currency appreciate. Which of the following *best* describes the adjustment that must occur if currency appreciation is to be effective in reducing the trade surplus?
    A. Domestic investment must decline relative to saving.
    B. Foreigners must increase investment relative to saving.
    C. Global capital flows must shift toward the domestic market.

CHAPTER **10**

CURRENCY EXCHANGE RATES: DETERMINATION AND FORECASTING

LEARNING OUTCOMES

After completing this chapter, you will be able to do the following:

- Calculate and interpret the bid/ask spread on a spot or forward foreign currency quotation and describe the factors that affect the bid/offer spread.
- Identify a triangular arbitrage opportunity and calculate its profit, given the bid/offer quotations for three currencies.
- Distinguish between spot and forward rates and calculate the forward premium or discount for a given currency.
- Calculate the mark-to-market value of a forward contract.
- Explain international parity relations—covered and uncovered interest rate parity, purchasing power parity, and the international Fisher effect.
- Describe relationships among the international parity conditions.
- Evaluate the use of the current spot rate, the forward rate, purchasing power parity, and uncovered interest parity to forecast future spot exchange rates.
- Explain approaches to assessing the long-run fair value of an exchange rate.
- Describe the carry trade and its relationship to uncovered interest rate parity, and calculate the profit from such a strategy.
- Explain how flows in the balance of payment accounts affect currency exchange rates.
- Describe the Mundell–Fleming model, the monetary approach, and the asset market (portfolio balance) approach to exchange rate determination.
- Forecast the direction of the expected change in an exchange rate based on balance of payment, Mundell–Fleming, monetary, and asset market approaches to exchange rate determination.
- Explain the potential impacts of monetary and fiscal policies on exchange rates.
- Describe the objectives and effectiveness of central bank intervention and capital controls.
- Describe warning signs of a currency crisis.
- Describe the use of technical analysis in forecasting exchange rates.

SUMMARY OVERVIEW

- Spot exchange rates apply to trades for the next settlement date (usually $T + 2$) for a given currency pair. Forward exchange rates apply to trades to be settled at any longer maturity.
- Market makers quote bid and offer prices (in terms of the *price currency*) at which they will buy or sell the *base currency*.
  - The offer price is always higher than the bid price.
  - The counterparty that asks for a two-sided price quote has the option (but not the obligation) to deal at either the bid or the offer price quoted.
  - The bid/offer spread depends on (1) the currency pair involved, (2) the time of day, (3) market volatility, (4) the transaction size, and (5) the relationship between the dealer and client. Spreads are tightest in highly liquid currency pairs (e.g., USD/EUR), when the key market centers (e.g., London) are open, and when market volatility is relatively low.
- Absence of arbitrage requires the following:
  - The bid shown by a dealer in the interbank market cannot be higher than the current interbank offer price, and the dealer's offer cannot be lower than the interbank bid.
  - The cross-rate bids posted by a dealer must be lower than the implied cross-rate offers available in the interbank market, and the dealer's offers must be higher than the cross-rate bids. If not, then a triangular arbitrage opportunity arises.
- Forward exchange rates are quoted in terms of points to be added to the spot exchange rate. If the points are positive (or negative), the base currency is trading at a forward premium (or discount). The points are proportional to the interest rate differential and approximately proportional to the time to maturity.
- Forecasting the direction of exchange rate movements can be a daunting task. Most studies find that models that work well in one period or for one set of exchange rates fail to work well for others.
- International parity conditions show us how expected inflation, interest rate differentials, forward exchange rates, and expected future spot exchange rates are linked in an ideal world. According to theory, relative expected inflation rates should determine relative nominal interest rates; relative interest rates, in turn, should determine forward exchange rates; and forward exchange rates should correctly anticipate the path of the future spot exchange rate.
- International parity conditions tell us that countries with high (or low) expected inflation rates should see their currencies depreciate (or appreciate) over time, that high-yield currencies should see their currencies depreciate relative to low-yield currencies over time, and that forward exchange rates should function as unbiased predictors of future spot exchange rates.
- With the exception of covered interest rate parity, which is enforced by arbitrage, the key international parity conditions rarely hold in either the short or the medium term. However, the parity conditions tend to hold over relatively long horizons.
- According to the theory of covered interest rate parity, an investment in a foreign-currency-denominated money market investment that is completely hedged against exchange rate risk in the forward market should yield exactly the same return as an otherwise identical domestic money market investment.
- According to the theory of uncovered interest rate parity, the expected change in a domestic currency's value should be fully reflected in domestic–foreign interest rate spreads. If the uncovered interest rate parity condition always held, it would rule out the possibility of earning excess returns from going long a high-yield currency and short a low-yield currency.

- According to the *ex ante* purchasing power parity condition, expected changes in exchange rates should equal the difference in expected national inflation rates.
- Most studies find that high-yield currencies do not depreciate and low-yield currencies do not strengthen as much as yield spreads would suggest over short- to medium-term periods. Many investors exploit this anomaly by engaging in so-called carry trades that overweight high-yield currencies at the expense of low-yield currencies. Historically, such carry trades have generated attractive excess returns in benign market conditions but tend to perform poorly when market conditions are highly volatile (i.e., they are subject to crash risk).
- If both *ex ante* purchasing power parity and uncovered interest rate parity held, real interest rates across all markets would be the same. This is real interest rate parity. Combining real interest rate parity with the fact that each country's nominal interest rate equals its real interest rate plus its expected inflation rate, we have the international Fisher effect: the nominal interest rate differential between two currencies equals the difference between the expected inflation rates.
- If both covered and uncovered interest rate parity held, the market would set the forward exchange rate equal to the spot exchange rate that is expected to prevail in the future. That is, the forward exchange rate would serve as an unbiased predictor of the future spot exchange rate.
- The purchasing power parity (PPP) approach to assessing long-run fair value probably has the widest following among international economists.
- The macroeconomic balance approach to assessing long-run fair value in the foreign exchange market estimates how much exchange rates will need to adjust to bring a country's current account balance to a sustainable level.
- The external debt sustainability approach to assessing long-run fair value in the foreign exchange market estimates what exchange rate level will ensure that a country's net external asset or liability position stabilizes at a viable level.
- A useful model of longer-term exchange rate determination can be obtained by combining convergence to a long-run equilibrium real exchange rate with uncovered interest rate parity:

$$q_{f/d} = \overline{q}_{f/d} + [(r_d - r_f) - (\varphi_d - \varphi_f)]$$

- For the most part, countries that run persistent current account deficits will see their currencies weaken over time. Similarly, countries that run persistent current account surpluses will tend to see their currencies appreciate over time.
- The relationship between current account imbalances and changes in exchange rates is not contemporaneous. Indeed, large current account imbalances can persist for long periods of time before they trigger an adjustment in exchange rates.
- A significant adjustment in exchange rates is often required to facilitate correction of a large current account gap. Many studies find long lags, perhaps lasting several years, between (1) the onset of the exchange rate change and (2) the adjustment in traded goods prices in response to the change in the exchange rate, and then (3) the eventual effect of the change in traded goods prices on import and export demand.
- Greater financial integration of the world's capital markets and the increased freedom of capital to flow across national borders have increased the importance of global capital flows in determining exchange rates.
- Countries that run relatively tight monetary policies, introduce structural economic reforms, and lower outsized budget deficits will often see their currencies strengthen over time as capital flows respond positively to relatively high nominal interest rates, lower

inflation expectations, a lower risk premium, and an upward revision in the market's assessment of what exchange rate level constitutes long-run fair value.

- Monetary policy affects the exchange rate through a variety of channels. In the Mundell–Fleming model, it does so primarily through the interest rate sensitivity of capital flows, strengthening the currency when monetary policy is tightened and weakening it when monetary policy is eased. The more sensitive capital flows are to the change in interest rates, the greater the exchange rate's responsiveness to the change in monetary policy.

- In the monetary model of exchange rate determination, monetary policy is deemed to have a direct impact on the actual and expected path of inflation, which, via purchasing power parity, translates into a corresponding impact on the exchange rate.

- Although monetary policy impulses may be transmitted to exchange rates through a variety of channels, the end result is broadly the same—countries that pursue overly easy monetary policies will see their currencies depreciate over time. If a central bank wishes to slow or reverse a decline in the value of its currency, a move toward a tighter monetary policy would be helpful, if not required.

- Fiscal policy has an ambiguous impact on the exchange rate. In the Mundell–Fleming model, an expansionary fiscal policy typically results in a rise in domestic interest rates and an increase in economic activity. The rise in domestic interest rates should induce a capital inflow, which is positive for the domestic currency, but the consequent rise in economic activity should contribute to a deterioration of the trade balance, which is negative for the domestic currency. The more mobile capital flows are, the greater the likelihood that the induced inflow of capital will dominate the deterioration in trade.

- Under conditions of high capital mobility, countries that simultaneously pursue expansionary fiscal policies and relatively tight monetary policies should see their currencies strengthen over time.

- The portfolio balance model of exchange rate determination asserts that a steady increase in the stock of government debt outstanding, perhaps generated by a steady widening of the government budget deficit over time, will be willingly held by investors only if they are compensated in the form of a higher expected return The higher expected return could come from (1) higher interest rates and/or higher risk premiums, (2) depreciation of the currency to a level sufficient to generate anticipation of gains from subsequent currency appreciation, or (3) some combination of the two.

- Surges in capital inflows can be a curse if they fuel boomlike conditions, asset price bubbles, and an overshoot of exchange rates into overvalued territory. One of the major issues confronting policy makers in emerging market countries is how best to respond to excessive surges in capital flows.

- The International Monetary Fund now considers capital controls to be a legitimate part of a policy maker's tool kit. Given the painful lessons from previous episodes of surging capital flows, the IMF feels that under certain circumstances, capital controls may be needed to prevent exchange rates from overshooting, asset price bubbles from forming, and future financial conditions from deteriorating.

- The evidence indicates that intervention by industrial countries has had an insignificant impact on the course of exchange rates. The evidence is more mixed for emerging markets. Emerging market policy makers might have greater success in managing their exchange rates given their large arsenal of foreign exchange reserve holdings, which appear sizable relative to the limited turnover of FX transactions in many emerging markets.

- Although each currency crisis episode is distinct in some respects, an IMF study of 50 episodes found the following stylized facts:
  - Leading up to a crisis, the real exchange rate is substantially higher than its mean level during tranquil periods.
  - The trade balance does not signal an impending currency crisis.
  - Foreign exchange reserves tend to decline precipitously as the crisis approaches.
  - On average, the terms of trade deteriorate somewhat leading up to a crisis.
  - Inflation tends to be significantly higher in precrisis periods.
  - The ratio of M2 (a measure of money supply) to bank reserves tends to rise in the 24-month period leading up to a crisis, then plummets sharply in the months immediately following a crisis.
  - Broad money growth in nominal and real terms tends to rise sharply in the two years leading up to a currency crisis, peaking around 18 months before a crisis hits.
  - Nominal private credit growth tends to rise sharply in the period leading up to a crisis.
  - Currency crises are often preceded by a boom–bust cycle in financial asset (equity) prices.
  - Real economic activity does not display any distinctive pattern ahead of a crisis but falls sharply in the aftermath of a crisis.
- Technical analysis is a popular trading tool for many, if not most, FX market participants. Numerous academic studies conducted in the 1970s, 1980s, and early 1990s concluded that a variety of trend-following trading rules would have generated significant profits had such models been actively followed during that period. However, updated studies for the post-1995 period indicate that trend-following trading rules have not fared as well since.
- Although technical analysis may now be less useful as a strategic tool to enhance return, a number of studies show that technical analysis may be a useful tool in managing the downside risk associated with FX portfolios.
- Most studies find that there exists a strong positive, *contemporaneous* relationship between cumulative order flow and exchange rates over short periods of time. However, the evidence is more mixed regarding whether order flow has *predictive* value for exchange rates.
- Empirical studies find that neither the data on currency risk reversals nor data on the size and trend in reported net speculative positions on the futures market are useful for currency forecasting purposes.

PRACTICE PROBLEMS

The following information relates to Questions 1 through 6.[1]

Ed Smith is a new trainee in the foreign exchange (FX) services department of a major global bank. Smith's focus is to assist the senior FX trader, Feliz Mehmet, CFA. Mehmet mentions that an Indian corporate client exporting to the United Kingdom wants to estimate the potential hedging cost for a sale closing in one year. Smith is to determine the premium or

---

[1]These practice problems were developed by Greg Gocek, CFA (Downers Grove, Illinois, USA).

discount for an annual (360-day) forward contract using the exchange rate data presented in Exhibit A:

Exhibit A: Select Currency Data for GBP and INR

Spot (INR/GBP)	79.5093
Annual (360-day) LIBOR (GBP)	5.43%
Annual (360-day) LIBOR (INR)	7.52%

Mehmet is also looking at two possible trades to determine their profit potential. The first trade involves a possible triangular arbitrage trade using the Swiss, U.S., and Brazilian currencies, to be executed based on a dealer's bid/offer rate quote of 0.5161/0.5163 in CHF/ BRL and the interbank spot rate quotes presented in Exhibit B:

Exhibit B: Interbank Market Quotes

Currency Pair	Bid/Offer
CHF/USD	0.9099/0.9101
BRL/USD	1.7790/1.7792

Mehmet is also considering a carry trade involving the USD and the euro. He anticipates it will generate a higher return than buying a one-year domestic note at the current market quote due to low U.S. interest rates and his predictions of exchange rates in one year. To help Mehmet assess the carry trade, Mehmet provides Smith with selected current market data and his one-year forecasts in Exhibit C:

Exhibit C: Spot Rates and Interest Rates for Proposed Carry Trade

Today's One-Year LIBOR		Currency Pair (Price/Base)	Spot Rate Today	Projected Spot Rate in One Year
USD	0.80%	CAD/USD	1.0055	1.0006
CAD	1.71%	EUR/CAD	0.7218	0.7279
EUR	2.20%			

Finally, Mehmet asks Smith to assist with a trade involving a U.S. multinational customer operating in Europe and Japan. The customer is a very cost-conscious industrial company with an AA credit rating and strives to execute its currency trades at the most favorable bid/offer spread. Because its Japanese subsidiary is about to close on a major European acquisition in three business days, the client wants to lock in a trade involving the Japanese yen and the euro as early as possible the next morning, preferably by 8:05 a.m. New York time.

At lunch, Smith and other FX trainees discuss how best to analyze currency market volatility from ongoing financial crises. The group agrees that a theoretical explanation of exchange rate movements, such as the framework of the international parity conditions, should be applicable across all trading environments. They note such analysis should enable traders to anticipate future spot exchange rates. But they disagree on which parity condition best predicts exchange rates, voicing several different assessments. Smith concludes the discussion on parity conditions by stating to the trainees:

"I believe that in the current environment both covered and uncovered interest rate parity conditions are in effect."

The conversation next shifts to exchange rate assessment tools, specifically the techniques of the IMF Consultative Group on Exchange Rate Issues (CGER). CGER uses a three-part approach that includes the macroeconomic balance approach, the external sustainability approach, and a reduced-form econometric model. Smith asks Leslie Jones, another trainee, to describe the three approaches. In response, Jones makes the following statements to the other trainees and Smith:

Statement 1: "The macroeconomic balance approach focuses on the stocks of outstanding assets and liabilities."
Statement 2: "The reduced-form econometric model has a weakness in underestimating future appreciation of undervalued currencies."
Statement 3: "The external sustainability approach centers on adjustments leading to long-term equilibrium in the capital account."

1. Based on Exhibit A, the forward premium or discount for a 360-day INR/GBP forward contract is *closest* to:
   A. −1.546.
   B. 1.546.
   C. 1.576.

2. Based on Exhibit B, the *most* appropriate recommendation regarding the triangular arbitrage trade is to:
   A. decline the trade, as no arbitrage profits are possible.
   B. execute the trade; buy BRL in the interbank market and sell it to the dealer.
   C. execute the trade; buy BRL from the dealer and sell it in the interbank market.

3. Based on Exhibit C, the potential all-in USD return on the carry trade is *closest* to:
   A. 1.04 percent.
   B. 1.40 percent.
   C. 1.84 percent.

4. The factor *least likely* to lead to a narrow bid/offer spread for the industrial company's needed currency trade is:
   A. the timing of its trade.
   B. the company's credit rating.
   C. the pair of currencies involved.

5. If Smith's statement on parity conditions is correct, future spot exchange rates are *most likely* to be forecast by:
   A. current spot rates.
   B. forward exchange rates.
   C. inflation rate differentials.

6. Which of the following statements given by trainee Jones in describing the approaches used by CGER is *most* accurate?
   A. Statement 1
   B. Statement 2
   C. Statement 3

The following information relates to Questions 7 through 13.[2]

Connor Wagener, a student at the University of Canterbury in New Zealand, has been asked to prepare a presentation on foreign exchange rates for his international business course. Wagener has a basic understanding of exchange rates, but would like a practitioner's perspective, and he has arranged an interview with currency trader Hannah McFadden. During the interview, Wagener asks McFadden:

"Could you explain what drives exchange rates? I'm curious as to why our New Zealand dollar was affected by the European debt crisis in 2011 and what other factors impact it."

In response, McFadden begins with a general discussion of exchange rates. She notes that international parity conditions illustrate how exchange rates are linked to expected inflation, interest rate differences, and forward exchange rates as well as current and expected future spot rates. McFadden states:

Statement 1: "Fortunately, the international parity condition most relevant for FX carry trades does not always hold."

McFadden continues her discussion:

"FX carry traders go long (i.e., buy) high-yield currencies and fund their positions by shorting—that is, borrowing in—low-yield currencies. Unfortunately, crashes in currency values can occur, which create financial crises as traders unwind their positions. For example, in 2008, the New Zealand dollar was negatively impacted when highly leveraged carry trades were unwound. In addition to investors, consumers and business owners can also affect currency exchange rates through their impact on their country's balance of payments. For example, if New Zealand consumers purchase more goods from China than New Zealand businesses sell to China, New Zealand will run a trade account deficit with China."

---

[2]These practice problems were developed by Sue Ryan, CFA (East Hartford, Connecticut, USA).

McFadden further explains:

Statement 2: "A trade surplus will tend to cause the currency of the country in surplus to appreciate, whereas a deficit will cause currency depreciation. Exchange rate changes will result in immediate adjustments in the prices of traded goods as well as in the demand for imports and exports. These changes will immediately correct the trade imbalance."

McFadden next addresses the influence of monetary and fiscal policy on exchange rates:

"Countries also exert significant influence on exchange rates both through the initial mix of their fiscal and monetary policies and also by subsequent adjustments to those policies. Various models have been developed to identify how these policies affect exchange rates. The Mundell-Fleming model addresses how changes in both fiscal and monetary policies affect interest rates and ultimately exchange rates in the short term."

McFadden describes monetary models by stating:

Statement 3: "Monetary models of exchange rate determination focus on the effects of inflation, price level changes, and risk premium adjustments."

McFadden continues her discussion:

"So far, we've touched on balance of payments and monetary policy. The portfolio balance model addresses the impacts of sustained fiscal policy on exchange rates. I must take a client call, but will return shortly. In the meantime, here is some relevant literature on the models I mentioned along with a couple of questions for you to consider."

Question 1: Assume an emerging market (EM) country has restrictive monetary and fiscal policies under low capital mobility conditions. Are these policies likely to lead to currency appreciation or currency depreciation, or to have no impact?

Question 2: Assume a developed market (DM) country has an expansive fiscal policy under high capital mobility conditions. Why is its currency most likely to depreciate in the long run under an integrated Mundell-Fleming and portfolio balance approach?

Upon her return, Wagener and McFadden review the questions. McFadden notes that capital flows can have a significant impact on exchange rates and have contributed to currency crises in both EM and DM countries. She explains that central banks, like the Reserve Bank of New Zealand, use FX market intervention as a tool to manage exchange rates. McFadden states:

Statement 4: "Some studies have found that EM central banks tend to be more effective in using exchange rate invention than DM central banks, primarily because of one important factor."

McFadden continues her discussion:

> **Statement 5:** "I mentioned that capital inflows could cause a currency crisis, leaving fund managers with significant losses. In the period leading up to a currency crisis, I would predict that an affected country's:
>
> **Prediction 1:** foreign exchange reserves will increase."
>
> **Prediction 2:** broad money growth in nominal and real terms will increase."
>
> **Prediction 3:** real exchange rate will be substantially higher than its mean level during tranquil periods."

After the interview, McFadden agrees to meet the following week with Wagener to discuss more recent events affecting the New Zealand dollar.

7. The international parity condition McFadden is referring to in Statement 1 is:
   A. purchasing power parity.
   B. covered interest rate parity.
   C. uncovered interest rate parity.

8. In Statement 2, McFadden is *most likely* failing to consider:
   A. the initial gap between the country's imports and exports.
   B. the price elasticity of export demand versus import demand.
   C. the lag in the response of import and export demand to price changes.

9. The *least* appropriate factor used to describe the type of models mentioned in Statement 3 is:
   A. inflation.
   B. price level changes.
   C. risk premium adjustments.

10. The best response to Question 1 is that the policies will:
   A. have no impact.
   B. lead to currency appreciation.
   C. lead to currency depreciation.

11. The most likely response to Question 2 is a(n):
   A. increase in the price level.
   B. decrease in risk premiums.
   C. increase in government debt.

12. The factor that McFadden is *most likely* referring to in Statement 4 is:
   A. FX reserve levels.
   B. domestic demand.
   C. the level of capital flows.

13. Which of McFadden's predictions in Statement 5 is *least* correct?
   A. Prediction 1
   B. Prediction 2
   C. Prediction 3

CHAPTER 11

ECONOMIC GROWTH AND THE INVESTMENT DECISION

LEARNING OUTCOMES

After completing this chapter, you will be able to do the following:

- Describe and compare factors favoring and limiting economic growth in developed and developing economies.
- Describe the relationship between the long-run rate of stock market appreciation and the sustainable growth rate of the economy.
- Explain the importance of potential gross domestic product (GDP) and its growth rate in the investment decisions of equity and fixed-income investors.
- Distinguish between capital-deepening investment and technological process and explain the impact of each on economic growth and labor productivity.
- Forecast potential GDP based on growth accounting relations.
- Explain the impact of natural resources on economic growth, and evaluate the argument that limited availability of natural resources constrains economic growth.
- Explain the effects of demographics, immigration, and labor force participation on the rate and sustainability of economic growth.
- Explain how investment in physical capital, human capital, and technological development affects economic growth.
- Compare classical growth theory, neoclassical growth theory, and endogenous growth theory.
- Explain and evaluate convergence hypotheses.
- Explain the economic rationale for governments to provide incentives to private investment in technology and knowledge.
- Describe the expected impact of removing trade barriers on capital investment and profits, employment and wages, and growth in the economies involved.

SUMMARY OVERVIEW

- The sustainable rate of economic growth is measured by the rate of increase in the economy's productive capacity or potential GDP.
- Growth in real GDP measures how rapidly the total economy is expanding. Per capita GDP, defined as real GDP divided by population, measures the standard of living in each country.

- The growth rate of real GDP and the level of per capita real GDP vary widely among countries. As a result, investment opportunities differ by country.
- Equity markets respond to anticipated growth in earnings. Higher sustainable economic growth should lead to higher earnings growth and equity market valuation ratios, all other things being equal.
- The best estimate for the long-term growth in earnings for a given country is the estimate of the growth rate in potential GDP.
- In the long run, the growth rate of earnings cannot exceed the growth in potential GDP. Labor productivity is critical because it affects the level of the upper limit. A permanent increase in productivity growth will raise the upper limit on earnings growth and should translate into faster long-run earnings growth and a corresponding increase in stock price appreciation.
- For global fixed-income investors, a critical macroeconomic variable is the rate of inflation. One of the best indicators of short- to intermediate-term inflation trends is the difference between the growth rate of actual and potential GDP.
- Capital deepening, an increase in the capital-to-labor ratio, occurs when the growth rate of capital (net investment) exceeds the growth rate of labor. In a graph of output per capita versus the capital-to-labor ratio, it is reflected by a move along the curve (i.e., the production function).
- An increase in total factor productivity (TFP) causes a proportional upward shift in the entire production function.
- One method of measuring sustainable growth uses the production function and the growth accounting framework developed by Solow. It arrives at the growth rate of potential GDP by estimating the growth rates of the economy's capital and labor inputs plus an estimate of total factor productivity.
- An alternative method measures potential growth as the long-term growth rate of the labor force plus the long-term growth rate of labor productivity.
- The forces driving economic growth include the quantity and quality of labor and the supply of non-ICT and ICT capital, public capital, raw materials, and technological knowledge.
- The labor supply is determined by population growth, the labor force participation rate, and net immigration. The physical capital stock in a country increases with net investment. The correlation between long-run economic growth and the rate of investment is high.
- Technological advances are discoveries that make it possible to produce more or higher-quality goods and services with the same resources or inputs. Technology is a major factor determining TFP. TFP is the main factor affecting long-term, sustainable economic growth rates in developed countries and also includes the cumulative effects of scientific advances, applied research and development, improvements in management methods, and ways of organizing production that raise the productive capacity of factories and offices.
- Total factor productivity, estimated using a growth accounting equation, is the residual component of growth once the weighted contributions of all explicit factors (e.g., labor and capital) are accounted for.
- Labor productivity is defined as output per worker or per hour worked. Growth in labor productivity depends on capital deepening and technological progress.
- The academic growth literature is divided into three theories—the classical view, the neoclassical model, and the new endogenous growth view.
- In the classical model, growth in per capita income is only temporary because an exploding population with limited resources brings per capita income growth to an end.
- In the neoclassical model, a sustained increase in investment increases the economy's growth rate only in the short run. Capital is subject to diminishing marginal returns, so

long-run growth depends solely on population growth, progress in TFP, and labor's share of income.

- The neoclassical model assumes that the production function exhibits diminishing marginal productivity with respect to any individual input.
- The point at which capital per worker and output per worker are growing at equal, sustainable rates is called the steady state or balanced growth path for the economy. In the steady state, total output grows at the rate of labor force growth plus the rate of growth of TFP divided by the elasticity of output with respect to labor input.
- The following parameters affect the steady state values for the capital-to-labor ratio and output per worker: saving rate, labor force growth, growth in TFP, depreciation rate, and elasticity of output with respect to capital.
- The main criticism of the neoclassical model is that it provides no quantifiable prediction of the rate or form of TFP change. TFP progress is regarded as exogenous to the model.
- Endogenous growth theory explains technological progress within the model rather than treating it as exogenous. As a result, self-sustaining growth emerges as a natural consequence of the model and the economy does not converge to a steady state rate of growth that is independent of saving/investment decisions.
- Unlike the neoclassical model, where increasing capital will result in diminishing marginal returns, the endogenous growth model allows for the possibility of constant or even increasing returns to capital in the aggregate economy.
- In the endogenous growth model, expenditures made on R&D and for human capital may have large positive externalities or spillover effects. Private spending by companies on knowledge capital generates benefits to the economy as a whole that exceed the private benefit to the company.
- The convergence hypothesis predicts that the rates of growth of productivity and GDP should be higher in the developing countries. Those higher growth rates imply that the per capita GDP gap between developing and developed economies should narrow over time. The evidence on convergence is mixed.
- Countries fail to converge because of low rates of investment and savings, lack of property rights, political instability, poor education and health, restrictions on trade, and tax and regulatory policies that discourage work and investing.
- Opening an economy to financial and trade flows has a major impact on economic growth. The evidence suggests that more open and trade-oriented economies will grow at a faster rate.

PRACTICE PROBLEMS

The following information refers to Questions 1 through 6.[1]

Hans Schmidt, CFA, is a portfolio manager with a boutique investment firm that specializes in sovereign credit analysis. Schmidt's supervisor asks him to develop estimates for GDP growth for three countries. Information on the three countries is provided in Exhibit A.

---

[1]These practice problems were developed by Karen Ashby, CFA (LaGrange, Kentucky, USA).

EXHIBIT A   Select Economic Data for Countries A, B, C

Country	Economy	Capital per Worker
A	Developed	High
B	Developed	High
C	Developing	Low

After gathering additional data on the three countries, Schmidt shares his findings with colleague, Sean O'Leary. After reviewing the data, O'Leary notes the following observations:

Observation 1: The stock market of Country A has appreciated considerably over the past several years. Also, the ratio of corporate profits to GDP for Country A has been trending upward over the past several years, and is now well above its historical average.

Observation 2: The government of Country C is working hard to bridge the gap between its standard of living and the living standards of developed countries. Currently, the rate of potential GDP growth in Country C is high.

Schmidt knows that a large part of the analysis of sovereign credit is to develop a thorough understanding of what the potential GDP growth rate is for a particular country and the region in which the country is located. Schmidt is also doing research on Country D for a client of the firm. Selected economic facts on Country D are provided in Exhibit B.

EXHIBIT B   Select Economic Facts for Country D

- Slow GDP growth
- Abundant natural resources
- Developed economic institutions

Prior to wrapping up his research, Schmidt schedules a final meeting with O'Leary to see if he can provide any other pertinent information. O'Leary makes the following statements to Schmidt:

Statement 1: "Many countries that have the same population growth rate, savings rate, and production function will have growth rates that converge over time."

Statement 2: "Convergence between countries can occur more quickly if economies are open and there is free trade and international borrowing and lending; however, there is no permanent increase in the rate of growth in an economy from a more open trade policy."

1. Based on Exhibit A, the factor that would *most likely* have the greatest positive impact on the per capita GDP growth of Country A is:
   A. free trade.
   B. technology.
   C. saving and investment.

2. Based on Observation 1, in the long run the ratio of profits to GDP in Country A is *most likely* to:
   A. remain near its current level.
   B. increase from its current level.
   C. decrease from its current level.

3. Based on Observation 2, Country C is *most likely* to have:
   A. relatively low real asset returns.
   B. a relatively low real interest rate.
   C. a relatively high real interest rate.

4. Based on Exhibit B, the *least likely* reason for the current pace of GDP growth in Country D is:
   A. a persistently strong currency.
   B. strong manufacturing exports.
   C. strong natural resource exports.

5. The type of convergence described by O'Leary in Statement 1 is *best* described as:
   A. club convergence.
   B. absolute convergence.
   C. conditional convergence.

6. Which of the following growth models is *most* consistent with O'Leary's Statement 2?
   A. Classical
   B. Endogenous
   C. Neoclassical

The following information relates to Questions 7 through 15.[2]

Victor Klymchuk, the chief economist at ECONO Consulting (EC), is reviewing the long-term GDP growth of three countries over the recent decade. Klymchuk is interested in forecasting the long-term change in stock market value for each country. Exhibit C presents current country characteristics and historical information on selected economic variables for the three countries.

Klymchuk instructs an associate economist at EC to assist him in forecasting the change in stock market value for each country. Klymchuk reminds the associate:

> *Statement 1:* "Over short time horizons, percentage changes in GDP, the ratio of earnings to GDP, and the price-to-earnings ratio are important factors for describing the relationship between economic growth and stock prices. However, I am interested in a long-term stock market forecast."

---

[2]These practice problems were developed by Lou Lemos, CFA (Louisville, Kentucky, USA).

EXHIBIT C   Select Country Factors and Historical Economic Data, 2000–2010

Country Factors	Growth in Hours Worked (%)	Growth in Labor Productivity (%)	Growth in TFP (%)	Growth in GDP (%)
Country A • High level of savings and investment • Highly educated workforce • Low tariffs on foreign imports • Limited natural resources	0.9	2.4	0.6	3.3
Country B • Developed financial markets • Moderate levels of disposable income • Significant foreign direct and indirect investments • Significant natural resources	−0.3	1.6	0.8	1.3
Country C • Politically unstable • Limited property rights • Poor public education and health • Significant natural resources	1.8	0.8	−0.3	2.6

A client is considering investing in the sovereign debt of Country A and Country B and asks Klymchuk his opinion of each country's credit risk. Klymchuk tells the client:

Statement 2: "Over the next 10 years, I forecast higher potential GDP growth for Country A and lower potential GDP growth for Country B. The capital per worker is similar and very high for both countries, but per capita output is greater for Country A."

The client tells Klymchuk that Country A will offer 50-year bonds and that he believes the bonds could be a good long-term investment given the higher potential GDP growth. Klymchuk responds to the client by saying:

Statement 3: "After the next 10 years, I think the sustainable rate of economic growth for Country A will be affected by a growing share of its population over the age of 65, a declining percentage under age 16, and minimal immigration."

The client is surprised to learn that Country C, a wealthy, oil-rich country with significant reserves, is experiencing sluggish economic growth and asks Klymchuk for an explanation. Klymchuk responds by stating:

Statement 4: "While countries with access to natural resources are often wealthier, the relationship between resource abundance and economic growth is not clear. My analysis shows that the presence of a dominant natural resource (oil) in Country C is constraining growth. Interestingly, Country A has few natural resources, but is experiencing a strong rate of increase in per capita GDP growth."

Klymchuk knows that growth in per capita income cannot be sustained by pure capital deepening. He asks the associate economist to determine how important capital deepening is as a source of economic growth for each country. Klymchuk instructs the associate to use the data provided in Exhibit C.

Klymchuk and his associate debate the concept of convergence. The associate economist believes that developing countries, irrespective of their particular characteristics, will eventually equal developed countries in per capita output. Klymchuk responds:

> **Statement 5:** "Poor countries will converge to the income levels of the richest countries only if they make appropriate institutional changes."

7. Based on the country factors provided in Exhibit C, the country *most likely* to be considered a developing country is:
   A. Country A.
   B. Country B.
   C. Country C.

8. Based on Exhibit C, capital deepening as a source of growth was *most* important for:
   A. Country A.
   B. Country B.
   C. Country C.

9. Based on Klymchuk's Statement 1, over the requested forecast horizon, the factor that will *most likely* drive stock market performance is the percentage change in:
   A. GDP.
   B. the earnings-to-GDP ratio.
   C. the price-to-earnings ratio.

10. Based solely on the predictions in Statement 2, over the next decade Country B's sovereign credit risk will *most likely*:
   A. increase.
   B. decrease.
   C. not change.

11. Based on Statement 2, the difference in per capita output between Country A and Country B is *most likely* due to differences in:
   A. capital deepening.
   B. capital per worker.
   C. total factor productivity.

12. Based on Statement 3, after the next 10 years the growth rate of potential GDP for Country A will *most likely* be:
   A. lower.
   B. higher.
   C. unchanged.

13. Based on Statement 4 and Exhibit C, the sluggish economic growth in Country C is *least likely* to be explained by:
    A. limited labor force growth.
    B. export-driven currency appreciation.
    C. poorly developed economic institutions.

14. Based on Statement 4, the higher rate of per capita income growth in Country A is *least likely* explained by:
    A. the rate of investment.
    B. the growth of its population.
    C. the application of information technology.

15. The type of convergence described by Klymchuk in Statement 5 is *best* described as:
    A. club convergence.
    B. absolute convergence.
    C. conditional convergence.

The following information relates to Questions 16 through 21.[3]

At a recent international finance and economics conference in Bamako, Mali, Jose Amaral of Brazil and Lucinda Mantri of India are discussing how to spur their countries' economic growth. Amaral believes that growth can be bolstered by removing institutional impediments, and suggests several possibilities for Brazil: launching a rural literacy program, clarifying property rights laws, and implementing a new dividend tax on foreign investors.

Mantri responds that, for India, capital deepening will be more effective, and has proposed the following ideas: building a group of auto and textile factories in the southern states, developing a north-south and east-west highway network, and sponsoring a patent initiative.

In response, Amaral says to Mantri:

"Based on endogenous growth theory, one of those proposals is more likely to raise total factor productivity than result in pure capital deepening."

While Mantri recognizes that India lacks the significant natural resources of Brazil, she states that India can overcome this challenge by bolstering long-term growth through three channels:

Channel 1: Deepening the capital base.
Channel 2: Making investments in technology.
Channel 3: Maintaining a low rupee exchange rate.

Each country's basic economic statistics were presented at the conference. Selected data for Brazil and India are shown in Exhibit D. Adama Kanté, a fund manager based in Mali, is

---

[3]These practice problems were developed by E. Shepard Farrar, CFA (Washington, D.C., USA).

planning to increase the fund's allocation to international equities, and, after some preliminary analysis, has determined that the new allocation will be to Brazilian or Indian equities. After reviewing the data in Exhibit D, Kanté decides that the allocation will be to Indian equities.

EXHIBIT D   Economic Statistics, Brazil and India

Economic Statistic	Brazil	India
GDP per capita, 2010	$9,589	$3,575
GDP per capita growth, 1990–2010	1.62%	4.84%
GDP growth, 2005–2008	4.9%	8.2%
Growth due to labor productivity component	2.9%	6.0%
Growth due to capital deepening component	3.4%	3.6%

Kanté is concerned about the low standard of living in Mali. To improve per capita GDP, Kanté is considering five specific strategies:

Strategy 1: Lower the country's tax rate.
Strategy 2: Introduce policies that encourage the return of highly educated Malian emigrants.
Strategy 3: Build day care centers to permit greater participation of women in the workforce.
Strategy 4: Impose high tariffs on imports to protect the country's nascent industries.
Strategy 5: Use economic development bank loans to improve the country's transport and manufacturing infrastructure.

16. Which of Amaral's initiatives is *least likely* to achieve his stated growth objective?
    A. Dividend tax
    B. Rural literacy
    C. Property rights

17. Which proposal for India is Amaral *most likely* referring to in his response to Mantri?
    A. Patent initiative
    B. Highway network
    C. Auto and textile factories

18. The channel that is *least likely* to help India overcome its challenge of lacking significant natural resources is:
    A. Channel 1.
    B. Channel 2.
    C. Channel 3.

19. Based on Exhibit D, which Indian economic statistic is *least likely* to support Kanté's international equity allocation preference?
    A. GDP per capita
    B. Growth due to labor productivity
    C. Growth due to capital deepening

20. The strategy that is *least likely* to improve per capita GDP in Mali is:
    A. Strategy 1.
    B. Strategy 2.
    C. Strategy 3.

21. Which of the following strategies being considered by Kanté is *most likely* to undermine or delay convergence with developed economies?
    A. Strategy 2
    B. Strategy 4
    C. Strategy 5

CHAPTER 12

ECONOMICS
OF REGULATION

LEARNING OUTCOMES

After completing this chapter, you will be able to do the following:

- Describe classifications of regulations and regulators.
- Describe uses of self-regulation in financial markets.
- Describe the economic rationale for regulatory intervention.
- Describe regulatory interdependencies and their effects.
- Describe tools of regulatory intervention in markets.
- Explain purposes in regulating commerce and financial markets.
- Describe anticompetitive behaviors targeted by antitrust laws globally, and evaluate the antitrust risk associated with a given business strategy.
- Describe benefits and costs of regulation.
- Evaluate effects on an industry, company, or security of a specific regulation.

SUMMARY OVERVIEW

- Legislative bodies, regulatory bodies, and courts typically enact regulation.
- Regulatory bodies include government agencies and independent regulators granted authority by a government or governmental agency. Some independent regulators may be self-regulating organizations.
- Typically, legislative bodies enact broad laws or statutes; regulatory bodies issue administrative regulations, often implementing statutes; and courts interpret statutes and administrative regulations, and these interpretations may result in judicial law.
- Regulators have responsibility for both substantive and procedural laws. The former focuses on rights and responsibilities of entities and relationships among entities. The latter focuses on the protection and enforcement of the former.
- The existence of informational frictions and externalities creates a need for regulation. Regulation is expected to have societal benefits and should be assessed using cost-benefit analysis.
- Regulation that arises to enhance the interests of regulated entities reflects regulatory capture.

- Regulatory competition is competition among different regulatory bodies to use regulation in order to attract certain entities.
- Regulatory arbitrage is the use of regulation by an entity to exploit differences in economic substance and regulatory interpretation or in regulatory regimes to the entity's benefit.
- Interdependence in the actions and potentially conflicting objectives of regulators is an important consideration for regulators, those regulated, and those assessing the effects of regulation.
- There are many regulatory tools available to regulators, including price mechanisms (such as taxes and subsidies), regulatory mandates and restrictions on behaviors, provision of public goods, and public financing of private projects.
- The choice of regulatory tool should be consistent with maintaining a stable regulatory environment. Stable does not mean unchanging, but rather refers to desirable attributes of regulation, including predictability, effectiveness in achieving objectives, time consistency, and enforceability.
- The breadth of regulation of commerce necessitates the use of a framework that identifies potential areas of regulation. This framework can be referenced to identify specific areas of regulation, existing and anticipated, that may affect the entity of interest.
- The regulation of securities markets and financial institutions is extensive and complex because of the consequences of failures in the financial system. These consequences include financial losses, loss of confidence, and disruption of commerce.
- The focus of regulators in financial markets includes prudential supervision, financial stability, market integrity, and economic growth, among others.
- Regulators—in assessing regulation and regulatory outcomes—should conduct ongoing cost-benefit analyses, develop techniques to enhance the measurement of these analyses, and use economic principles for guidance.
- Net regulatory burden to the entity of interest is an important consideration for an analyst.

PRACTICE PROBLEMS

The following information relates to Questions 1 through 6.[1]

Tiu Asset Management (TAM) recently hired Jonna Yun. Yun is a member of TAM's Global Equity portfolio team and is assigned the task of analyzing the effects of regulation on the U.S. financial services sector. In her first report to the team, Yun makes the following statements:

> *Statement 1:* "The Dodd-Frank Wall Street Reform and Consumer Protection Act (Dodd-Frank Act), enacted on 21 July 2010 by the U.S. Congress, will have a significant effect on U.S. banks and other financial services firms."
>
> *Statement 2:* "The U.S. Securities and Exchange Commission (SEC) allocates certain regulatory responsibilities to the Financial Industry Regulatory Authority (FINRA), with the goal of ensuring that the securities industry operates fairly and honestly."
>
> *Statement 3:* "The Dodd-Frank Act called for derivatives reforms, including shifting from bilateral to centralized derivatives settlement, by July 2011. The G-20 called for

---

[1] These practice problems were developed by E. Shepard Farrar, CFA (Washington, D.C., USA).

action by its members on derivatives reform by year-end 2012. The accelerated time line of the Dodd-Frank Act concerned some U.S. firms."

Statement 4: "Regulators use various tools to intervene in the financial services sector."

Statement 5: "Regulations may bring benefits to the U.S. economy, but they may also have unanticipated costly effects."

Statement 6: "Regulation Q imposed a ceiling on interest rates paid by banks for certain bank deposits."

1. The *most* appropriate classification of the Dodd-Frank Act, referred to in Statement 1, is a(n):
   A. statute.
   B. judicial law.
   C. administrative law.

2. The Financial Industry Regulatory Authority, referred to in Statement 2, is *best* classified as a:
   A. legislative body.
   B. government agency.
   C. self-regulatory organization.

3. What is the *most likely* basis for the concerns noted in Statement 3?
   A. Externalities
   B. Regulatory arbitrage
   C. Informational friction

4. The tools *least likely* to be used by regulators to intervene in financial markets are:
   A. blackout periods.
   B. capital requirements.
   C. insider trading restrictions.

5. Which of the following is *most likely* an unanticipated effect of regulation?
   A. Hiring compliance lawyers
   B. Setting legal standards for contracts
   C. Establishing employers' rights and responsibilities

6. After Regulation Q was imposed, the demand for money market funds *most likely*:
   A. increased.
   B. decreased.
   C. remained unchanged.

PART II

SOLUTIONS

CHAPTER 1

DEMAND AND SUPPLY ANALYSIS: INTRODUCTION

SOLUTIONS

1. A is correct. Coats are finished goods, the result of the output of production.
2. B is correct.
3. C is correct. In order to draw demand and supply curves, own price and own quantity must be allowed to vary. However, all other variables are held constant to focus on the relationship of own price with quantity.
4. B is correct. Producers generally will supply a greater quantity of a good at higher prices for the good.
5. C is correct. Because the supply curve is the graph of the inverse supply function, solve for the inverse supply function given the wage rate of 11:

$$Q_x^s = -4 + \tfrac{1}{2}P_x - 2(11)$$
$$= -26 + \tfrac{1}{2}P_x$$
$$Q_x^s + 26 = \tfrac{1}{2}P_x$$
$$P_x = 52 + 2Q_x^s$$

The vertical intercept is 52.
6. B is correct. The demand curve shows quantity demanded as a function of own price only.
7. B is correct. The positive coefficient on the unit price of aluminum implies that aluminum is a substitute for steel. Thus, an increase in the price of aluminum implies that more steel can be sold at given price for steel than before, as steel is substituted for aluminum.
8. A is correct. The slope coefficient of Q_s^s in the inverse supply function is 0.04.

$$\text{Start with the supply equation: } Q_s^s = -55 + 26P_s + 1.3P_a$$
$$\text{Insert } P_a = 10: \quad = -55 + 26P_s + 1.3(10)$$
$$= -42 + 26P_s$$
$$\text{Solve for } P_s: \quad P_s = 1.6 + 0.04Q_s^s \text{(the inverse supply function)}$$

9. B is correct. Start with the equation $Q_s^i = -55 + 26P_s + 1.3P_a$. To aggregate for five suppliers, multiply the individual producer's supply function by 5:

$$Q_s^i = 5(-55 + 26P_s + 1.3P_a)$$
$$Q_s^i = -275 + 130P_s + 6.5P_a$$

Now insert the unit price of aluminum at 20:

$$Q_s^i = -275 + 130P_s + 6.5(20)$$
$$Q_s^i = -145 + 130P_s$$

Invert the equation to get the market inverse supply function:

$$P_s = 1.1 + 0.008Q_s^i$$

10. A is correct. At market equilibrium the quantity demanded just equals the quantity supplied; thus, the difference between the two is zero.
11. A is correct. Excess supply at a given price implies that there is not enough demand at that price. So the price must fall until it reaches the point at which the demand and supply curves intersect.
12. A is correct. The basic Dutch auction is a descending-price auction.
13. B is correct. Noncompetitive bids and bidders at lower yields will get their orders filled first. Securities may then not be available to fill demand entirely at the highest winning yield.
14. A is correct. The winning bidder in such auctions may be overly optimistic about the underlying value of the item won.
15. A is correct. The situation described is one of excess demand because, in order for markets to clear at the given level of quantity supplied, the company would need to raise prices.
16. A is correct. The lowest acceptable price to the supplier at any given quantity must now increase because part of the price is paid as a per-unit tax. Thus, the supply curve shifts upward.
17. C is correct. A deadweight loss is the surplus lost by both the producer and the consumer and not transferred to anyone.
18. C is correct. The trade price should be the same whether the tax is imposed on the buyer or on the seller.
19. C is correct. A quota will cause excess demand, raising the price of the good and moving it up and to the left along the demand curve. This should shift some of the buyer's surplus to the seller.
20. B is correct. We find consumer surplus as the area of the triangle formed by the y (price) axis, the inverse demand curve, and a line segment from the y axis to the inverse demand function at $P = 10$.
    Put the price into the demand equation:

$$Q^d = 50 - 0.75(10)$$
$$Q^d = 42.5 \text{ (this is the base of the triangle)}$$

Invert the demand function by solving for P:

$$-0.75P = Q^d - 50$$
$$P = -1.33Q^d + 66.67$$

Note the price intercept is 66.67. The height of the triangle is $66.67 - 10 = 56.67$. The consumer surplus is the area of the triangle above the price of 10 and below the demand curve, with base equal to the quantity of 42.5: ½ Base × Height = $(½)(42.5)$ $(66.7 - 10) = 1{,}205$.

21. A is correct. Producer surplus is the difference between the total revenue that sellers receive from selling a given amount of a good and the total variable cost of producing that amount.

22. A is correct. With a linear supply curve, producer surplus is equal to the area of a triangle with base equal to the market-clearing price minus the price intercept, height equal to the market-clearing quantity, and bounded by the supply curve as the hypotenuse. Given a (market-clearing) price of 15, quantity is 2:

$$Q_s = -7 + 0.6(15) = 2$$

Next find the inverse supply function: $P = (1/0.6)7 + (1/0.6)Q_s$

$$P = 11.67 + 1.67 Q_s$$

Note that the price intercept is 11.7 and the quantity intercept is −7.0. Thus, producer surplus is ½ Base × Height = $(½)(2)(15 - 11.7) = 3.3$.

23. B is correct. From the demand function:

$$\Delta Q_{pr}^d / \Delta P_{pr} = -3.1 (\text{the coeffient in front of own price})$$

$$\text{Solve for } Q_{pr}^d: \ Q_{pr}^d = 84 - 3.1 P_{pr} + 0.8I + 0.9 P_{pu}$$

$$= 84 - 3.1(38) + 0.8(100) + 0.9(18)$$

$$= 62.4$$

$$\text{At } P_{pr} = 38, \ \text{price elasticity of demand} = (\Delta Q_{pr}^d / \Delta P_{pr})(P_{pr}/Q_{pr}^d)$$

$$= (-3.1)(38/62.4)$$

$$= -1.9$$

24. C is correct. From the demand function:

$$\Delta Q_{pr}^d / \Delta I = 0.8 \ (\text{coefficient in front of the income variable})$$

$$\text{Solve for } Q_{pr}^d: \ Q_{pr}^d = 84 - 3.1 P_{pr} + 0.8I + 0.9 P_{pu}$$

$$= 84 - 3.1(38) + 0.8(100) + 0.9(18)$$

$$= 62.4$$

$$\text{At } I = 100, \ \text{the income elasticity of demand} = (\Delta Q_{pr}^d / \Delta I)(I/Q_{pr}^d)$$

$$= (0.8)(100/62.4)$$

$$= 1.3$$

25. A is correct. From the demand function:

$$\Delta Q_{pr}^d / \Delta P_{pu} = 0.9 \,(\text{the coefficient in front of } P_{pu})$$

$$\text{Solve for } Q_{pr}^d\!: Q_{pr}^d = 84 - 3.1 P_{pr} + 0.8I + 0.9 P_{pu}$$

$$= 84 - 3.1(38) + 0.8(100) + 0.9(18)$$

$$= 62.4$$

At $P_{pr} = 38$ and $P_{pu} = 18$, the cross-price elasticity of demand

$$= (\Delta Q_{pr}^d / \Delta P_{pu})(P_{pu} / Q_{pr}^d)$$

$$= (0.9)(18/62.4)$$

$$= 0.3$$

26. C is correct. With complements, consumption goes up or down together. With a negative cross-price elasticity, as the price of one good goes up, the demand for both falls.

CHAPTER 2

DEMAND AND SUPPLY ANALYSIS: CONSUMER DEMAND

SOLUTIONS

1. C is correct. If the child prefers the zoo over the park and the beach over the zoo, then she should prefer the beach over the park according to the axiom of transitive preferences.
2. B is correct. Utility functions only allow ordinal rankings of consumer preferences.
3. C is correct. The slope of the indifference curve at any point gives the marginal rate of substitution of one good for another. The curve is convex because the marginal value of one good versus another decreases the more one has of the first good.
4. C is correct. The marginal rate of substitution is equal to the negative of the slope of the tangent to the indifference curve at that point, or -2.
5. B is correct. Maximum utility is achieved where the highest attainable indifference curve intersects with just one point (the tangency) on the budget constraint line.
6. A is correct. In the case of normal goods, the income and substitution effects are reinforcing, leading to an increase in the amount purchased after a drop in price.
7. A is correct. The income effect overwhelms the substitution effect such that an increase in the price of the good results in greater demand for the good, resulting in a positively sloped demand curve.
8. A is correct. Veblen goods are not inferior goods, whereas Giffen goods are. An increase in income for consumers of a Veblen good leads to an increase in the quantity purchased at each price. The opposite is true for a Giffen good.

CHAPTER 3

DEMAND AND SUPPLY ANALYSIS: THE FIRM

SOLUTIONS

1. A is correct. Normal profit is the level of accounting profit such that implicit opportunity costs are just covered; thus, it is equal to a level of accounting profit such that economic profit is zero.

2. B is correct. Economic rent results when a commodity is fixed in supply (highly inelastic) and the market price is higher than what is required to bring the commodity to market. An increase in demand in this circumstance would result in a rising price and increased potential for economic rent.

3. B is correct. Profit is the return to entrepreneurship for its contribution to the economic process.

4. A is correct. Marginal revenue per unit is defined as the change in total revenue divided by the change in quantity sold. $MR = \Delta TR \div \Delta Q$. In this case, change in total revenue equals CHF100,000, and change in total units sold equals 50. CHF100,000 ÷ 50 = CHF2,000.

5. A is correct. In a perfectly competitive market, an increase in supply by a single firm will not affect price. Therefore, an increase in units sold by the firm will be matched proportionately by an increase in revenue.

6. A is correct. Marginal revenue per unit is defined as the change in total revenue divided by the change in quantity sold. $MR = \Delta TR \div \Delta Q$. In this case, change in total revenue per day equals €3,000 [(450 × €40) − (300 × €50)], and change in units sold equals 150 (450 − 300). €3,000 ÷ 150 = €20.

7. A is correct. Under perfect competition, a firm is a price taker at any quantity supplied to the market, and $AR = MR =$ Price.

8. A is correct. Average fixed cost is equal to total fixed cost divided by quantity produced: $AFC = TFC/Q = 200/4 = 50$.

9. C is correct. Marginal cost is equal to the change in total cost divided by the change in quantity produced. $MC = \Delta TC/\Delta Q = 80/1 = 80$.

10. C is correct. Average total cost is equal to total cost divided by quantity produced. At five units produced, the average total cost is 104. $ATC = TC/Q = 520/5 = 104$.

11. A is correct. Under perfect competition, price equals marginal revenue. A firm breaks even when marginal revenue equals average total cost.

12. C is correct. The firm should shut down production when marginal revenue is less than average variable cost.

13. B is correct. When total revenue is enough to cover variable costs but not total fixed costs in full, the firm can survive in the short run but would be unable to maintain financial solvency in the long run.

14. A is the correct choice. The quantity at which average total cost is minimized does not necessarily correspond to a profit maximum.

15. C is correct. Output increases in the same proportion as input increases occur at constant returns to scale.

16. C is correct. The firm operating at greater than long-run efficient scale is subject to diseconomies of scale. It should plan to decrease its level of production.

17. A is correct. Competition should drive prices down to long-run marginal cost, resulting in only normal profits being earned.

18. B is correct. The development and extraction of scarce oil and gas represent an increasing-cost industry. A positive shift in demand will cause firms to increase supply, but at higher costs. The higher costs associated with increasing supply will cause prices to rise.

19. A is correct. A positive shift in demand will cause firms to increase supply, but at decreasing costs. The decreasing cost per unit will be passed on to consumers and cause prices to fall in the long run.

20. A is correct. Three workers produce the highest average product equal to 170. $AP = 510/3 = 170$.

21. B is correct. Marginal product is equal to the change in total product divided by the change in labor. The increase in MP from two to three workers is 190: $MP = \Delta TP/\Delta L = (510 - 320)/(3 - 2) = 190/1 = 190$.

22. A is correct. Adding new workers in numbers sufficient for them to specialize in their roles and functions should increase marginal product of labor.

23. C is correct. Costs are minimized when substitution of labor for capital (or the reverse) does not result in any cost savings, which is the case when the marginal product per dollar spent is equalized across inputs.

24. B is correct. An expansion in production by 200 units can be achieved by two unskilled workers at a total cost of $400, or $2 per unit produced. $400/200 = $2 per unit produced.

25. B is correct. The firm employs labor of various types in a cost-minimizing combination. Profit is maximized when marginal revenue product is equalized across each type of labor input. If the wage rate of unskilled workers increases, the marginal product produced per dollar spent to employ unskilled labor will decline. The original employment mix is no longer optimal, so the firm will respond by shifting away from unskilled workers to workers whose wages are unaffected by the minimum wage law.

26. C is correct. The marginal revenue product is the marginal product of an additional craftsperson (10 chairs) times the price per chair (€100). $10 \times €100 = €1,000$.

27. B is correct. The marginal revenue product for additional power tools is €1,000, which exceeds the €800 cost of the tools by €200. $(10 \times €100 = €1,000) - €800 = €200$.

THE FIRM AND MARKET STRUCTURES

SOLUTIONS

1. C is correct. Monopolistic competition is characterized by many sellers, differentiated products, and some pricing power.
2. A is correct. A market structure with few sellers of a homogeneous or standardized product characterizes an oligopoly.
3. B is the correct choice. The product produced in a perfectly competitive market cannot be differentiated by advertising or any other means.
4. C is correct. Profits are maximized when MR = MC. For a monopoly, MR = $P[1 - 1/E_p]$. Setting this equal to MC and solving for P:

$$\$40 = P[1 - 1/1.5] = P * 0.333$$
$$P = \$120$$

5. B is correct. The long-run competitive equilibrium occurs where MC = AC = P for each company. Equating MC and AC implies $2 + 8Q = 256/Q + 2 + 4Q$.

   Solving for Q gives $Q = 8$. Equating MC with price gives $P = 2 + 8Q = 66$. Any price above 66 yields an economic profit because $P =$ MC > AC, so new companies will enter the market.
6. B is correct. A company in a perfectly competitive market must accept whatever price the market dictates. The marginal cost schedule of a company in a perfectly competitive market determines its supply function.
7. A is correct. As prices decrease, smaller companies will leave the market rather than sell below cost. The market share of Aquarius, the price leader, will increase.
8. C is correct. In the Nash model, each company considers the other's reaction in selecting its strategy. In equilibrium, neither company has an incentive to change its strategy. ThetaTech is better off with open architecture regardless of what SigmaSoft decides. Given this choice, SigmaSoft is better off with a proprietary platform. Neither company will change its decision unilaterally.
9. C is correct. The profit-maximizing choice is the level of output where marginal revenue equals marginal cost.

10. A is correct. The oligopolist faces two different demand structures, one for price increases and another for price decreases. Competitors will lower prices to match a price reduction, but will not match a price increase. The result is a kinked demand curve.

11. B is the correct choice. When companies have similar market shares, competitive forces tend to outweigh the benefits of collusion.

12. B is correct. The economic profit will attract new entrants to the market and encourage existing companies to expand capacity.

13. B is correct. The dominant company's market share tends to decrease as profits attract entry by other companies.

14. B is correct. This allows the investors to receive a normal return for the risk they are taking in the market.

15. B is correct. The top four companies in the industry comprise 86 percent of industry sales: $(300 + 250 + 200 + 150)/(300 + 250 + 200 + 150 + 100 + 50) = 900/1,050 = 86\%$.

16. B is correct. The three-firm Herfindahl-Hirschman index is $0.35^2 + 0.25^2 + 0.20^2 = 0.225$.

17. B is correct. The Herfindahl-Hirschman index does not reflect low barriers to entry that may restrict the market power of companies currently in the market.

18. B is correct. The credible threat of entry holds down prices and multiple incumbents are offering undifferentiated products.

19. C is correct. There are many competitors in the market, but some product differentiation exists, as the price differential between Deep River's brand and the house brands indicates.

CHAPTER 5

AGGREGATE OUTPUT, PRICES, AND ECONOMIC GROWTH

SOLUTIONS

1. B is correct. GDP is the total amount spent on all final goods and services produced within the economy over a specific period of time.
2. C is the correct choice. By-products of production processes that have no explicit market value are not included in GDP.
3. C is the correct choice. Government transfer payments, such as unemployment compensation or welfare benefits, are excluded from GDP.
4. A is correct. Canadian GDP is the total market value of all final goods and services produced in a given time period within Canada. The wine produced in Canada counts toward Canadian GDP.
5. B is correct. This is the value added by the artist: £5,000 − £2,000 = £3,000.
6. B is correct. The GDP deflator = Nominal GDP/Real GDP. To get a ratio less than 1, real GDP exceeds nominal GDP, which indicates that prices have decreased and, accordingly, deflation has occurred.
7. A is correct. Nominal GDP is defined as the value of goods and services measured at current prices. The term *expenditures* is used synonymously with *the value of goods and services* since aggregate expenditures must equal aggregate output of an economy.
8. B is correct. Real GDP in the first year was €100 billion/1.11 = €90 and in the last year it was €300 billion/2.00 = €150. Thus, (€150 − €90)/€90 = 0.67 or 67%.
9. A is correct: $(212.8/190)^{1/2} - 1 = 0.0583$ or 5.8%.
10. B is correct.

$$\text{GDP deflator} = \frac{\text{Value of current-year output at current-year prices}}{\text{Value of current-year output at base-year prices}} \times 100$$

11. B is correct. GDP = Consumption + Gross private domestic investment + Government spending + Exports − Imports = 15 + 4 + 3.8 + 1.5 − 1.7 = 22.6. National income = GDP − CCA − Statistical discrepancy = 22.6 − 1.5 − 0.5 = 20.6.
12. C is the correct choice. Unincorporated business net income is also known as proprietor's income and is included in personal income.

13. A is the correct choice. The fundamental relationship among saving, investment, the fiscal balance, and the trade balance is $S = I + (G - T) + (X - M)$. This form of the relationship shows that private saving must fund investment expenditures, the government fiscal balance, and net exports (= net capital outflows). Rearranging gives $G - T = (S - I) - (X - M)$. The government's fiscal deficit $(G - T)$ must be equal to the private sector's saving/investment balance $(S - I)$ minus net exports.

14. C is correct. The fundamental relationship among saving, investment, the fiscal balance, and the trade balance is $S = I + (G - T) + (X - M)$. Given the levels of output and investment spending, an increase in saving (reduction in consumption) must be offset by either an increase in the fiscal deficit or an increase in net exports. Increasing the fiscal deficit is not one of the choices, so an increase in net exports and corresponding increase in net capital outflow (increased lending to foreigners and/or increased purchases of assets from foreigners) is the correct response.

15. A is correct. The IS curve represents combinations of income and the real interest rate at which planned expenditure equals income.

16. B is correct. The IS curve represents combinations of income and the real interest rate at which planned expenditure equals income. Equivalently, it represents combinations such that

$$S(Y) = I(r) + (G - T) + (X - M)$$

where $S(Y)$ indicates that planned saving is an increasing function of income and $I(r)$ indicates that planned investment is a decreasing function of the real interest rate. To maintain this relationship, an increase in government spending (G) requires an increase in saving at any given level of the interest rate (r). This implies an increase in income (Y) at each interest rate level—a rightward shift of the IS curve. Unless the LM curve is vertical, the IS and LM curves will intersect at a higher level of aggregate expenditure/income. Since the LM curve embodies a constant price level, this implies an increase in aggregate expenditure at each price level—a rightward shift of the aggregate demand curve.

17. C is correct. The LM curve represents combinations of income and the interest rate at which the demand for real money balances equals the supply. For a given price level, an increase in the nominal money supply is also an increase in the real money supply. To increase the demand for real money balances, either the interest must decline or income must increase. Therefore, at each level of the interest rate, income (= expenditure) must increase—a rightward shift of the LM curve. Since the IS curve is downward sloping (higher income requires a lower interest rate), a rightward shift in the LM curve means that the IS and LM curves will intersect at a higher level of aggregate expenditure/income. This implies a higher level of aggregate expenditure at each price level—a rightward shift of the aggregate demand curve.

18. B is correct. The LM curve represents combinations of income and the interest rate at which the demand for real money balances equals the supply. For a given nominal money supply, an increase in the price level implies a decrease in the real money supply. To decrease the demand for real money balances, either the interest must increase or income must decrease. Therefore, at each level of the interest rate, income (= expenditure) must decrease—a leftward shift of the LM curve.

19. A is correct. A decrease in the price level increases the real money supply and shifts the LM curve to the right. Since the IS curve is downward sloping, the IS and LM curves will intersect at a higher level of income and a lower interest rate.

20. C is correct. At the full employment, or natural, level of output the economy is operating at an efficient and unconstrained level of production. Companies have enough spare capacity to avoid bottlenecks, and there is a modest, stable pool of unemployed workers (job seekers equal job vacancies) looking for and transitioning into new jobs.

21. C is correct. Due to long-term contracts and other rigidities, wages and other input costs do not fully adjust to changes in the price level in the short run. Given input prices, firms respond to output price changes by expanding or contracting output to maximize profit. Hence, the SRAS is upward sloping.

22. B is correct. The slope of the short-run aggregate supply curve reflects the extent to which wages and other input costs adjust to the overall price level. Automatic adjustment of wages would mitigate the impact of price changes on profitability. Hence, firms would not adjust output as much in response to changing output prices—the SRAS curve would be steeper.

23. B is the correct choice. A weak domestic currency will result in an increase in aggregate demand at each price level—a rightward shift in the AD curve. A weaker currency will cause a country's exports to be cheaper in global markets. Conversely, imports will be more expensive for domestic buyers. Hence, the net exports component of aggregate demand will increase.

24. B is correct. Productivity measures the efficiency of labor and is the amount of output produced by workers in a given period of time. A decline in productivity implies decreased efficiency. A decline in productivity increases labor costs, decreases profitability, and results in lower output at each output price level—a leftward shift in both the short-run and the long-run aggregate supply curves.

25. C is correct. The wealth effect explains the impact of increases or decreases in household wealth on economic activity. Household wealth includes financial and real assets. As asset values increase, consumers save less and spend more out of current income since they will still be able to meet their wealth accumulation goals. Therefore, an increase in household wealth results in a rightward shift in the aggregate demand curve.

26. B is correct. Higher aggregate demand (AD) and higher aggregate supply (AS) raise real GDP and lower unemployment, meaning employment levels increase.

27. A is the correct choice. Stagflation occurs when output is declining and prices are rising. This is most likely due to a decline in aggregate supply—a leftward shift of the SRAS curve. Depending on the source of the shift, the LRAS may shift, too.

28. B is correct. An increase in energy prices will shift the short-run aggregate supply curve (SRAS) to the left, reducing output and increasing prices. If there is no change in the aggregate demand curve, in particular if the central bank does not expand the money supply, slack in the economy will put downward pressure on input prices, shifting the SRAS back to its original position. In the long run, the price level will be unchanged.

29. A is correct. Technology is the most important factor affecting economic growth for developed countries. Technological advances are very important because they allow an economy to overcome the limits imposed by diminishing marginal returns.

30. B is correct. Labor productivity can be directly measured as output per hour.

31. B is correct. The sustainable growth rate is equal to the growth rate of the labor force plus the growth rate of labor productivity (i.e., output per worker). Unlike total factor productivity, output per worker is observable, so this is the most practical way to approach estimation of sustainable growth.

32. B is correct. Total factor productivity (TFP) is a scale factor primarily reflecting technology. An increase in TFP means that output increases for any level of factor inputs.

33. B is correct. The estimated equation is the standard Solow growth accounting equation. The intercept is the growth rate of total factor productivity.

34. C is correct. In the standard Solow growth accounting equation, the coefficient on each factor's growth rate is its share of income.

35. B is correct. Diminishing marginal productivity of capital means that as a country accumulates more capital per worker the incremental boost to output declines. Thus, all else being the same, economies grow more slowly as they become more capital intensive. Given the relative scarcity and hence high marginal productivity of capital in developing countries, they tend to grow more rapidly than developed countries. This leads to convergence in income levels over time.

CHAPTER 6

UNDERSTANDING BUSINESS CYCLES

SOLUTIONS

1. C is correct. Business cycles relate to fluctuations in national economic activity generated mainly through business enterprises.
2. B is correct. The stages of the business cycle occur repeatedly over time.
3. B is correct. The net trend during contraction is negative.
4. A is correct. Inflation is rising at economic peaks.
5. C is correct. At the end of a recession, firms will run lean production to generate maximum output with the fewest number of workers.
6. B is correct. Physical capital adjustments to downturns come through aging of equipment plus lack of maintenance.
7. C is correct. Near the top of a cycle, sales begin to slow before production is cut, leading to an increase in inventories relative to sales.
8. A is correct. Austrian economists see monetary policy mistakes as leading to booms and busts.
9. A is correct. Monetarists caution that policy effects can occur long after the need for which they were implemented is no longer an issue.
10. B is correct. Discouraged workers are defined as persons who have stopped looking for work and are outside the labor force.
11. C is correct. This effect makes unemployment rise more slowly as recessions start and fall more slowly as recoveries begin.
12. A is correct. The impact of new technologies can be experienced over a period as long as decades, whereas unemployment is measured over a much shorter time frame.
13. B is correct. With inflation, a fixed amount of money buys fewer goods and services, thus reducing purchasing power.
14. C is correct. Disinflation is known as a reduction of inflation from a higher to lower, but still above-zero, level.
15. B is correct. Deflation is connected to a vicious cycle of reduced spending and higher unemployment.
16. A is the correct choice. In hyperinflation, consumers accelerate their spending to beat price increases, and money circulates more rapidly.

17. A is correct. The Laspeyres index is calculated with these inputs:
    - November consumption bundle: $70 \times 0.9 + 60 \times 0.6 = 99$
    - December consumption bundle: $70 \times 1 + 60 \times 0.8 = 118$
    - December price index: $(118/99) \times 100 = 119.19$
    - Inflation rate: $(119.19/100) - 1 = 0.1919 = 19.19\%$

18. A is correct. The Paasche index uses the current product mix of consumption combined with the variation of prices. So for December, its value is

$$(120 \times 1 + 50 \times 0.8)/(120 \times 0.9 + 50 \times 0.6) = (160/138) \times 100 = 115.9$$

19. C is correct. Central banks typically use consumer price indexes to monitor inflation and evaluate their monetary policies.

20. C is the correct choice. The CPI is typically used for this purpose, while the PPI is more closely connected to business contracts.

21. A is correct. Core inflation is less volatile since it excludes food and energy prices and therefore will not be as likely to lead to policy overreactions when serving as a target.

22. C is correct. For productivity (output per hour), the faster it can grow, the further wages can rise without putting pressure on business costs per unit of output.

23. C is correct. While no single indicator is definitive, a mix of them—which can be affected by various economic determinants—can offer the strongest signal of performance.

24. B is correct. The narrowing spread of Treasury yields and the federal funds rate, a leading indicator, foretells a drop in short-term rates and a fall in economic activity. The prime rate is a lagging indicator and typically moves after the economy turns.

25. A is correct. Both inventory-to-sales ratio and unit labor costs are lagging indicators that decline somewhat after a peak. Real personal income is a coincident indicator that by its decline shows a slowdown in business activity.

CHAPTER 7

MONETARY AND FISCAL POLICY

SOLUTIONS

1. B is correct. There is an inverse relationship between the money multiplier and the reserve requirement. The money multiplier is equal to 1 divided by the reserve requirement.

2. A is correct. Precautionary money demand is directly related to GDP. Precautionary money balances are held to provide a buffer against unforeseen events that might require money. Precautionary balances tend to rise with the volume and value of transactions in the economy, and therefore rise with GDP.

3. B is correct. When the interest rate on bonds is I_1 there is an excess supply of money (equal to $M_0 - M_1 > 0$). Economic agents would seek to buy bonds with their excess money balances, which would force the price of bonds up and the interest rate down to I_0.

4. A is the correct choice. According to the theory of money neutrality, an increase in the money supply ultimately leads to an increase in the price level and leaves real variables unaffected in the long run.

5. B is correct. If money were neutral in the short run, monetary policy would not be effective in influencing the economy.

6. B is correct. By definition, monetarists believe prices may be controlled by manipulating the money supply.

7. A is correct. The Fisher effect is based on the idea that the real interest rate is relatively stable. Changes in the nominal interest rate result from changes in expected inflation.

8. A is correct. The Fisher effect implies that changes in the nominal interest rate reflect changes in expected inflation, which is consistent with Nominal interest rate = Real interest rate + Expected rate of inflation.

9. C is correct. Unanticipated inflation has greater costs than anticipated inflation.

10. C is the correct choice. Transfer payment programs represent fiscal, not monetary policy.

11. B is the correct choice. The supervision of banks is not a role that all central banks assume. When it is a central bank's role, responsibility may be shared with one or more entities.

12. A is correct. Central bank activities are typically intended to maintain price stability. Concerning choice B, note that the transmission channels of monetary policy are not independent.

13. A is correct. Investment is expected to move inversely with the official policy rate.

14. A is the correct choice. Such action would tend to constrict the money supply and increase interest rates, all else held equal.

15. A is correct. The central bank described is target independent because it set its own targets (e.g., the target inflation rate) and operationally independent because it decides how to achieve its targets (e.g., the time horizon).

16. A is correct. Interest rates are expected to rise to protect the exchange rate target.

17. C is correct. The purchase of government bonds via open market operations increases banking reserves and the money supply; it is consistent with an expansionary monetary policy.

18. A is correct. The neutral rate of interest is that rate of interest that neither stimulates nor slows down the underlying economy. The neutral rate should be consistent with stable long-run inflation.

19. B is correct. A central bank would decrease an official interest rate to stimulate the economy. The setting in which an official interest rate is lowered to zero (the lowest value that could be targeted) without stimulating economic growth suggests that there are limits to monetary policy.

20. C is correct. Raising reserve requirements should slow money supply growth.

21. C is correct. Deflation poses a challenge to conventional monetary policy because once the central bank has cut nominal interest rates to zero to stimulate the economy, it cannot cut them further.

22. A is the correct choice. The inability to determine exactly the neutral rate of interest does not necessarily limit the power of monetary policy.

23. A is correct. Public financing of a power plant could be described as a fiscal policy tool to stimulate investment.

24. C is the correct choice. Ensuring stable purchasing power is a goal of monetary rather than fiscal policy. Fiscal policy involves the use of government spending and tax revenue to affect the overall level of aggregate demand in an economy and hence the level of economic activity.

25. A is correct. Monetary actions may face fewer delays to taking action than fiscal policy, especially when the central bank is independent.

26. B is correct. Cyclically adjusted budget deficits are appropriate indicators of fiscal policy. These are defined as the deficit that would exist if the economy was at full employment (or full potential output).

27. B is the correct choice. Fiscal policy is subject to recognition, action, and impact lags.

28. C is correct. A freeze in discretionary government spending is an example of a contractionary fiscal policy.

29. A is correct. A pay-as-you-go rule is a neutral policy because any increases in spending or reductions in revenues would be offset. Accordingly, there would be no net impact on the budget deficit or surplus.

30. B is correct. Quantitative easing is an example of an expansionary monetary policy stance. It attempts to spur aggregate demand by drastically increasing the money supply.

31. B is correct. The belief is that high levels of debt to GDP may lead to higher future tax rates, which may lead to disincentives to economic activity.

32. A is correct. Government borrowing may compete with private-sector borrowing for investment purposes.

33. A is correct. If both fiscal and monetary policies are easy, then the joint impact will be highly expansionary, leading to a rise in aggregate demand, low interest rates, and growing private and public sectors.

CHAPTER 8

INTERNATIONAL TRADE
AND CAPITAL FLOWS

SOLUTIONS

1. A is correct. Countries gain from exchange when trade enables each country to receive a higher price for exported goods and/or pay a lower price for imported goods. This leads to more efficient resource allocation and allows consumption of a larger variety of goods.

2. B is correct. Resources may need to be reallocated into or out of an industry, depending on whether that industry is an exporting sector or an import-competing sector of that economy. As a result of this adjustment process, less efficient companies may be forced to exit the industry, which in turn may lead to higher unemployment and the need for retraining in order for displaced workers to find jobs in expanding industries.

3. A is correct. The copper industry in Copperland would benefit from trade. Because the cost of producing copper relative to producing tea is lower in Copperland than in Tealand, Copperland will export copper and the industry will expand.

4. B is correct. Comparative advantage is present when the country's opportunity cost of producing a good is less than that of a trading partner.

5. C is correct. While Brazil has an absolute advantage in the production of both flashlights and vegetables, Mexico has a comparative advantage in the production of vegetables. The opportunity cost of vegetables in Mexico is ⅓ per flashlight, while the opportunity cost of vegetables in Brazil is 1.5 per flashlight.

6. C is correct. Mexico has the lowest opportunity cost to produce an extra ruler. The opportunity cost is two pencils per ruler in Mexico, three pencils per ruler in Brazil, and four pencils per ruler in China.

7. A is correct. In the Ricardian model, comparative advantage is determined by technology differences between countries. Technology determines output per worker in each industry in each country. Differences in technology between countries cause output per worker in each industry to differ between countries. These ratios determine the pattern of comparative advantage.

8. C is correct. A country gains if trade increases the price of its exports relative to its imports as compared to its autarkic prices; that is, the final terms of trade are more favorable than its autarkic prices. If the relative prices of exports and imports remain the same after trade opens, then the country will consume the same basket of goods before and after trade opens, and it gains nothing from the ability to trade. In that case, its trade partner will capture all of the gains. Of course, the opposite is true if the roles are reversed. More

generally, a country captures more of the gains from trade the more the final terms of trade differ from its autarkic prices.

9. A is correct. In the Heckscher–Ohlin model a country has a comparative advantage in goods whose production is intensive in the factor with which it is relatively abundantly endowed. In this case, capital is relatively abundant in Germany so Germany has a comparative advantage in producing the capital-intensive product: machine tools. Portugal is relatively labor abundant; hence it should produce and export the labor-intensive product: wine.

10. B is correct. As a country opens up to trade, doing so has a favorable impact on the abundant factor and a negative impact on the scarce factor. This is because trade causes the output mix to change and therefore changes the relative demand for the factors of production. Increased output of the export product increases demand for the factor that is used intensively in its production, while reduced output of the import product decreases demand for the factor used intensively in its production. Because the export product uses the abundant factor intensively and the import product uses the scarce factor intensively, the abundant factor gains relative to the scarce factor in each country.

11. A is correct. The imposition of a tariff will most likely increase domestic government revenue. A tariff is a tax on imports collected by the importing country's government.

12. C is correct. With a voluntary export restraint, the price increase induced by restricting the quantity of imports (= quota rent for equivalent quota = tariff revenue for equivalent tariff) accrues to foreign exporters and/or the foreign government.

13. A is correct. By definition, a large country is big enough to affect the world price of its imports and exports. A large country can benefit by imposing a tariff if its terms of trade improve by enough to outweigh the welfare loss arising from inefficient allocation of resources.

14. A is correct. A customs union extends a free trade area (FTA) by not only allowing free movement of goods and services among members, but also creating a common trade policy against nonmembers. Unlike a more integrated common market, a customs union does not allow free movement of factors of production among members.

15. C is correct. Regional trading agreements are politically less contentious and quicker to establish than multilateral trade negotiations (for example, under the World Trade Organization). Policy coordination and harmonization are easier among a smaller group of countries.

16. A is correct. The capital account measures capital transfers and sale and purchase of nonproduced, nonfinancial assets such as mineral rights and intangible assets.

17. B is correct. The current account measures the flows of goods and services (including income from foreign investments). Patent fees and legal services are both captured in the services subaccount of the current account.

18. C is correct. The current account includes income received on foreign investments. The South Korean company effectively exported the use of its capital during the quarter to its U.S. subsidiary, and the dividend represents payment for those services.

19. B is correct. A current account deficit tends to result from low private saving, high private investment, a government deficit, or a combination of the three. Of the choices, only low private savings contributes toward a current account deficit.

20. B is the correct choice. A current account deficit tends to result from low private saving, high private investment, a government deficit, or a combination of the three. Of these choices, only high investments can increase productive resources and improve future ability to repay creditors.

21. B is correct. The WTO provides the legal and institutional foundation of the multinational trading system and is the only international organization that regulates cross-border trade relations among nations on a global scale. The WTO's mission is to foster free trade by providing a major institutional and regulatory framework of global trade rules. Without such global trading rules, it would be hard to conceive of today's global transnational corporations.

22. A is correct. The World Bank's mission is to help developing countries fight poverty and enhance environmentally sound economic growth. The World Bank helps to create the basic economic infrastructure essential for creation and maintenance of domestic financial markets and a well-functioning financial industry in developing countries.

23. C is correct. From an investment perspective, the IMF helps to keep country-specific market risk and global systemic risk under control. The Greek sovereign debt crisis on 2010, which threatened to destabilize the entire European banking system, is a recent example. The IMF's mission is to ensure the stability of the international monetary system, the system of exchange rates and international payments that enables countries to buy goods and services from each other.

24. C is correct. The GATT was the only multilateral body governing international trade from 1948 to 1995. It operated for almost half a century as a quasi-institutionalized, provisional system of multilateral treaties and included several rounds of negotiations.

CHAPTER 9

CURRENCY
EXCHANGE RATES

SOLUTIONS

1. B is correct. The exchange rate is the number of units of the price currency that one unit of the base currency will buy. Equivalently, it is the number of units of the price currency required to buy one unit of the base currency.

2. B is correct. The real exchange rate (quoted in terms of domestic currency per unit of foreign currency) is given by:

$$\text{Real exchange rate}_{(d/f)} = S_{d/f} \times (P_f/P_d)$$

An increase in the domestic price level (P_d) *decreases* the real exchange rate because it implies an *increase* in the relative purchasing power of the domestic currency.

3. B is correct. The receivable is due in 100 days. To reduce the risk of currency exposure, the British company would initiate a forward contract to sell euros/buy pounds at an exchange rate agreed to today. The agreed-upon rate is called the forward exchange rate.

4. C is correct. The sell side generally consists of large banks that sell foreign exchange and related instruments to buy-side clients. These banks act as market makers, quoting exchange rates at which they will buy (the bid price) or sell (the offer price) the base currency.

5. B is correct. In the case of a direct exchange rate, the domestic currency is the price currency (the numerator) and the foreign currency is the base currency (the denominator). If the domestic currency appreciates, then fewer units of the domestic currency are required to buy one unit of the foreign currency, and the exchange rate (domestic per foreign) declines. For example, if sterling (GBP) appreciates against the euro (EUR), then euro–sterling (GBP/EUR) might decline from 0.8650 to 0.8590.

6. A is correct. An indirect quote takes the foreign country as the price currency and the domestic country as the base currency. To get CHF—which is the executive's domestic currency—as the base currency, the quote must be stated as EUR/CHF. Using the hotel manager's information, the indirect exchange rate is (1/1.2983) = 0.7702.

7. C is correct. The appreciation of sterling against the Swiss franc is simply the inverse of the 12 percent depreciation of the Swiss franc against sterling: $[1/(1 - 0.12)] - 1 = (1/0.88) - 1 = 0.1364$, or 13.64%.

8. B is correct. The percentage appreciation of the base currency can be calculated by dividing the appreciated exchange rate by the initial exchange rate. In this case, the unknown is the initial exchange rate. The initial exchange is the value of x that satisfies the formula:

$$1.4500/x = 1.08$$

Solving for x leads to $1.45/1.08 = 1.3426$.

9. A is correct. To get to the ZAR/HKD cross-rate, it is necessary to take the inverse of the CNY/ZAR spot rate and then multiply by the CNY/HKD exchange rate:

$$ZAR/HKD = (CNY/ZAR)^{-1} \times (CNY/HKD)$$
$$= (1/0.9149) \times 0.8422 = 0.9205$$

10. C is correct. The ZAR/SEK cross-rate from the original dealer is $(1.0218/0.9149) = 1.1168$, which is lower than the quote from the second dealer. To earn an arbitrage profit, a currency trader would buy SEK (sell ZAR) from the original dealer and sell SEK (buy ZAR) to the second dealer. On 1 million SEK the profit would be:

$$SEK1,000,00 \times (1.1210 - 1.1168) = ZAR4,200$$

11. B is correct. The number of forward points equals the forward rate minus the spot rate, or $0.14193 - 0.1378 = 0.00413$, multiplied by 10,000: $10,000 \times 0.00413 = 41.3$ points. By convention, forward points are scaled so that ± 1 forward point corresponds to a change of ± 1 in the last decimal place of the spot exchange rate.

12. A is correct. Given the forward rate and forward points as a percentage, the unknown in the calculation is the spot rate. The calculation is:

$$Spot\ rate \times (1 + Forward\ points\ as\ a\ percentage) = Forward\ rate$$
$$Spot\ rate \times (1 + 0.068) = 1.0123$$
$$Spot = 1.0123/1.068 = 0.9478$$

13. B is correct. The base currency trading at a forward discount means that one unit of the base currency costs less for forward delivery than for spot delivery; that is, the forward exchange rate is less than the spot exchange rate. The forward points, expressed either as an absolute number of points or as a percentage, are negative.

14. C is correct. To eliminate arbitrage opportunities, the spot exchange rate (S), the forward exchange rate (F), the interest rate in the base currency (i_b), and the interest rate in the price currency (i_p) must satisfy:

$$\frac{F}{S} = \left(\frac{1 + i_p}{1 + i_b}\right)$$

According to this formula, the base currency will trade at forward premium ($F > S$) if, and only if, the interest rate in the price currency is higher than the interest rate in the base currency ($i_p > i_b$).

15. B is correct. The forward exchange rate is given by:

$$F_{JPY/AUD} = S_{JPY/AUD}\left(\frac{1 + i_{JPY}T}{1 + i_{AUD}T}\right) = 82.42 \left[\frac{1 + 0.0015\left(\dfrac{90}{360}\right)}{1 + 0.0495\left(\dfrac{90}{360}\right)}\right]$$

$$= 82.42 \times 0.98815 = 81.443$$

The forward points are $100 \times (F - S) = 100 \times (81.443 - 82.42) = 100 \times (-0.977) = -97.7$. Note that because the spot exchange rate is quoted with two decimal places, the forward points are scaled by 100.

16. C is the correct choice. An ideal currency regime would have credibly fixed exchange rates among all currencies. This would eliminate currency-related uncertainty with respect to the prices of goods and services as well as real and financial assets.

17. C is correct. Fixed exchange rates impose severe limitations on the exercise of independent monetary policy. With a rigidly fixed exchange rate, the domestic interest rates, monetary aggregates (e.g., money supply), and credit conditions are dictated by the requirement to buy or sell the currency at the rigid parity. Even a narrow band around the parity level allows the monetary authority to exercise some discretionary control over these conditions. In general, the wider the band, the more independent control the monetary authority can exercise.

18. B is correct. With a currency board, the monetary authority is legally required to exchange domestic currency for a specified foreign currency at a fixed exchange rate. It cannot issue domestic currency without receiving foreign currency in exchange, and it must hold that foreign currency as a 100 percent reserve against the domestic currency issued. Thus, the country's monetary base (bank reserves plus notes and coins in circulation) is fully backed by foreign exchange reserves.

19. A is correct. A trade deficit must be exactly matched by an offsetting capital account surplus to fund the deficit. A capital account surplus reflects borrowing from foreigners (an increase in domestic liabilities) and/or selling assets to foreigners (a decrease in domestic assets). A capital account surplus is often referred to as a capital inflow because the net effect is foreign investment in the domestic economy.

20. A is correct. A devaluation of the domestic currency means domestic producers are cutting the prices faced by their foreign customers. The impact on their unit sales and their revenue depends on the elasticity of demand. Expensive luxury goods exhibit high price elasticity. Hence, luxury car producers are likely to experience a sharp increase in sales and revenue due to the devaluation.

21. C is correct. The trade surplus cannot decline unless the capital account deficit also declines. Regardless of the mix of assets bought and sold, foreigners must buy more assets from (or sell fewer assets to) domestic issuers/investors.

CHAPTER 10

CURRENCY EXCHANGE RATES: DETERMINATION AND FORECASTING

SOLUTIONS

1. C is correct. The equation to calculate the forward premium or discount is:

$$F_{f/d} - S_{f/d} = S_{f/d} \left[\frac{\left(\dfrac{\text{Actual}}{360}\right)}{1 + i_d \left(\dfrac{\text{Actual}}{360}\right)} \right] (i_f - i_d)$$

$S_{f/d}$ is the spot rate with GBP the base currency or d, and with INR the foreign currency or f. $S_{f/d}$ per Exhibit A is 79.5093, i_f is equal to 7.52 percent, and i_d is equal to 5.43 percent.

With GBP as the base currency (i.e., the domestic currency) in the INR/GBP quote, substituting in the relevant base currency values from Exhibit A yields the following:

$$F_{f/d} - S_{f/d} = 79.5093 \left[\frac{\left(\dfrac{360}{360}\right)}{1 + 0.0573 \left(\dfrac{360}{360}\right)} \right] (0.0752 - 0.0543)$$

$$F_{f/d} - S_{f/d} = 79.5093 \left(\frac{1}{1.0543}\right) (0.0752 - 0.0543)$$

$$F_{f/d} - S_{f/d} = 1.576$$

2. B is correct. The dealer is posting an offer rate to buy BRL at a price that is too high. This overpricing is determined by calculating the interbank implied cross-rate for the CHF/BRL using the intuitive equation-based approach:
CHF/BRL = CHF/USD × (BRL/USD)$^{-1}$, or
CHF/BRL = CHF/USD × USD/BRL

Inverting the BRL/USD given quotes in Exhibit B determines the USD/BRL bid/ offer rates of 0.56205/0.56211. (The bid of 0.56205 is the inverse of the BRL/USD offer, calculated as 1/1.7792; the offer of 0.56211 is the inverse of the BRL/USD bid, calculated as 1/1.7790.) Multiplying the CHF/USD and USD/BRL bid/offer rates then leads to the interbank implied CHF/BRL cross-rate of:

Bid: 0.9099 × 0.56205 = 0.5114

Offer: 0.9101 × 0.56211 = 0.5116

Since the dealer is willing to buy BRL at 0.5161 but BRL can be purchased from the interbank market at 0.5116, there is an arbitrage opportunity to buy BRL in the interbank market and sell it to the dealer for a profit of 0.0045 CHF (0.5161 − 0.5116) per BRL transacted.

3. A is correct. The carry trade involves borrowing in a lower-yielding currency to invest in a higher-yielding one and netting any profit after allowing for borrowing costs and exchange rate movements. The relevant trade is to borrow USD and lend in euros. To calculate the all-in USD return from a one-year EUR LIBOR deposit, first determine the current and one-year later USD/EUR exchange rates. Because one USD buys CAD 1.0055 today, and one CAD buys EUR 0.7218 today, today's EUR/USD rate is the product of these two numbers: 1.0055 × 0.7218 = 0.7258. The projected rate one year later is: 1.0006 × 0.7279 = 0.7283. Accordingly, measured in dollars, the investment return for the unhedged EUR LIBOR deposit is equal to:

$$(1.0055 \times 0.7218) \times (1 + 0.022) \times [1/(1.0006 \times 0.7279)]$$
$$= 0.7258 \times (1.022)(1/0.7283) = 1.0184 - 1 = 1.84\%$$

However, the borrowing costs must be charged against this *gross* return to fund the carry trade investment (one-year USD LIBOR was 0.80 percent). The *net* return on the carry trade is thereby closest to: 1.84% − 0.80% = 1.04%.

4. B is the correct choice. Although credit ratings can affect spreads, the trade involves spot settlement (i.e., two business days after the trade date), so the spread quoted to this highly rated (AA) firm is not likely to be much tighter than the spread that would be quoted to a somewhat lower-rated (but still high-quality) firm. The relationship between the bank and the client, the size of the trade, the time of day the trade is initiated, the currencies involved, and the level of market volatility are likely to be more significant factors in determining the spread for this trade.

5. B is correct. By rearranging the terms of the equation defining covered interest rate parity, and assuming that uncovered interest rate parity is in effect, the forward exchange rate is equal to the expected future spot exchange rate, $F_{f/d} = S^e_{f/d}$, with the expected percentage change in the spot rate equal to the interest rate differential. Thus, the forward exchange rate is an unbiased forecast of the future spot exchange rate.

6. C is correct. The external sustainability approach deals with stocks (i.e., levels) of outstanding assets or debt and the financial flows associated with the capital account. The comment correctly states the external sustainability approach focuses on adjustments resulting in long-term equilibrium in the capital account.

7. C is correct. The carry trade strategy is dependent upon the fact that uncovered interest rate parity does not hold in the short or medium term. If uncovered interest rate parity held, it would mean that investors would receive identical returns from either an unhedged foreign currency investment or a domestic currency investment because the

appreciation/depreciation of the exchange rate would offset the yield differential. However, during periods of low volatility, evidence shows that high-yield currencies do not depreciate enough and low-yield currencies do not appreciate enough to offset the yield differential.

8. C is correct. McFadden states that exchange rates will *immediately* correct the trade imbalance. She is describing the flow supply/demand channel, which assumes that trade imbalances will be corrected as the deficit country's currency depreciates, causing its exports to become more competitive and its imports to become more expensive. Studies indicate that there can be long lags between exchange rate changes, changes in the prices of traded goods, and changes in the trade balance. In the short run, exchange rates tend to be more responsive to investment and financing decisions.

9. C is the correct choice. Risk premiums are more closely associated with the portfolio balance approach. The portfolio balance approach addresses the impact of a country's net foreign asset/liability position. Under the portfolio balance approach, investors are assumed to hold a diversified portfolio of assets, including foreign and domestic bonds. Investors will hold a country's bonds as long as they are compensated appropriately. Compensation may come in the form of higher interest rates and/or higher risk premiums.

10. B is correct. The currency is likely to appreciate, not depreciate. The emerging market country has both a restrictive monetary policy and restrictive fiscal policy under conditions of low capital mobility. Low capital mobility indicates that interest rate changes induced by monetary and fiscal policy will not cause large changes in capital flows. Implementation of restrictive policies should result in an improvement in the trade balance, which will result in currency appreciation.

11. C is correct. Expansionary fiscal policies result in currency depreciation in the long run. Under a portfolio balance approach, the assumption is that investors hold a mix of domestic and foreign assets, including bonds. Fiscal stimulus policies result in budget deficits, which are often financed by debt. As the debt level rises, investors become concerned as to how the ongoing deficit will be financed. The country's central bank may need to create more money in order to purchase the debt, which would cause the currency to depreciate. Or the government could adopt a more restrictive fiscal policy, which would also depreciate the currency.

12. A is correct. EM countries are better able to influence their exchange rates because their reserve levels as a ratio to average daily FX turnover are generally much greater than those of DM countries. This means that EM central banks are in a better position to affect currency supply and demand than are DM countries, where the ratio is negligible. EM policy makers use their foreign exchange reserves as a kind of insurance to defend their currencies as needed.

13. A is correct. Prediction 1 is least likely to be correct. Foreign exchange reserves tend to decline precipitously, not increase, as a currency crisis approaches. Broad money growth in nominal and real terms tends to rise sharply in the two years leading up to a currency crisis, peaking around 18 months before a crisis hits. In the period leading up to a currency crisis, the real exchange rate is substantially higher than its mean level during tranquil periods.

CHAPTER 11

ECONOMIC GROWTH AND THE INVESTMENT DECISION

SOLUTIONS

1. B is correct. Country A is a developed country with a high level of capital per worker. Technological progress and/or more intensive use of existing technology can help developed countries increase productivity and thereby increase per capita GDP. Most developed countries have reasonably low trade barriers; thus, somewhat freer trade is likely to have only an incremental, and probably transitory, impact on per capita GDP growth. Also, since the country already has a high capital-to-labor ratio, increased saving/investment is unlikely to increase the growth rate substantially unless it embodies improved technology.

2. C is correct. The ratio of profits to GDP for Country A has been trending upward over the past several years, and is now well above its historical average. The ratio of profits to GDP cannot rise forever. At some point stagnant labor income would make workers unwilling to work without an increase in wages and would also undermine demand, making further expansion of profit margins unsustainable. Thus, it is likely that the ratio of profits to GDP will decline in the long run toward its historical average.

3. C is correct. A high growth rate of potential GDP would cause real incomes to rise more rapidly and also translate into higher real interest rates and higher expected/required real asset returns. The real interest rate is essentially the real return that consumers and savers demand in exchange for postponing consumption. Faster growth in potential GDP means that consumers expect their real incomes to rise more rapidly. This implies that an extra unit of future income/consumption is less valuable than it would be if incomes were expected to grow more slowly. All else held the same, the real interest rate will have to be relatively high in order to induce the savings required to fund required/desired capital accumulation.

4. B is the correct choice. Country D is a country with abundant resources and has developed the economic institutions necessary for growth, yet the country is experiencing slow economic growth. It is likely that Country D is experiencing the Dutch disease, where currency appreciation driven by strong export demand for natural resources makes other segments of the economy, in particular manufacturing, globally uncompetitive. Strong manufacturing exports would indicate that Country D is globally competitive and likely to have adopted leading-edge technology. Thus, it is unlikely that the slow growth reflects inability to maintain productivity growth. Similarly, strong exports would suggest

adequate demand for Country D's products. Thus, strong exports are unlikely to be the cause of slow growth.

5. C is correct. Conditional convergence means that convergence is conditional on the countries having the same savings rate, population growth rate, and production function. If these conditions hold, the neoclassical model implies convergence to the same *level* of per capita output as well as the same steady state growth rate.

6. C is correct. According to the neoclassical model, convergence should occur more quickly if economies are open and there is free trade and international borrowing and lending. Opening up the economy should increase the rate at which the capital-to-labor ratio converges among countries. However, in the neoclassical Solow model, after the reallocation of world savings, there is no permanent increase in the rate of growth in an economy. Both the developed and developing countries eventually grow at the same steady state rate.

7. C is correct. Country C is the most likely to be a developing economy. Political instability, limited property rights, and poor public education and health are all factors that limit economic growth, and thereby contribute to a relatively low standard of living.

8. A is correct. The associate economist can measure the effect of pure capital deepening by measuring the difference of the growth rates of labor productivity and total factor productivity (TFP). The larger the difference, the more important capital deepening is as a source of economic growth. From 2000 to 2010, Country A's labor productivity grew by 2.4 percent per year, of which 0.6 percent came from TFP growth and 1.8 percent from capital deepening (2.4% − 0.6% = 1.8%).

9. A is correct. In the long run, the growth rate of GDP is the most important driver of stock market performance. Therefore, the associate economist should focus on the drivers of long-run potential GDP growth. The ratio of earnings to GDP cannot increase indefinitely since that would imply that profit would eventually absorb all of GDP. This ratio cannot shrink forever, either, since unprofitable companies will go out of business. Thus, the annualized growth rate of the earnings-to-GDP ratio must be approximately zero over long time horizons and this ratio should not be a dominant factor in forecasting long-term stock market performance. Similarly, the price-to-earnings ratio cannot grow or contract at a finite rate forever, because investors will not pay an excessive price for each dollar of earnings, nor will they give away earnings for free. Therefore the rate of change in the price-to-earnings ratio must be approximately zero over long time horizons and should not be a dominant factor in the forecast of long-term stock market performance.

10. A is correct. Credit rating agencies consider the growth rate of potential GDP when evaluating the credit risk of sovereign debt. The chief economist's expectation of lower potential GDP growth for Country B over the next decade increases the perceived credit risk of its sovereign bonds.

11. C is correct. The higher per capita output for Country A is most likely due to differences in the cumulative impact of technological progress embodied in total factor productivity. Technological progress raises the productive capacity of a country. Technological progress causes an upward shift in the entire production function, resulting in higher output per worker for a given level of capital per worker.

12. A is correct. Demographic factors can positively or negatively contribute to a country's sustainable rate of economic growth. After the next 10 years, Country A is expected to experience a growing share of the population over the age of 65 and a declining percentage of the population under the age of 16. All else held the same, this implies slower growth of the labor force and hence slower growth of potential GDP. Immigration could offset these

demographic challenges. However, Statement 3 indicates that Country A is expected to experience minimal immigration.

13. A is the correct choice. Country C is an example of a country endowed with an abundant natural resource yet experiencing slow economic growth. While labor force growth is an important source of economic growth, it is the least likely explanation of the sluggish economic growth in Country C. As shown in Exhibit C, growth in total hours worked has accounted for most of Country C's growth. Furthermore, export-driven currency appreciation and poorly developed economic institutions are both likely causes of sluggish growth in countries with abundant natural resources.

14. B is the correct choice. Population growth can increase the growth rate of the overall economy, but does not impact the rate of increase in *per capita* GDP. Therefore, population growth does not explain Country A's higher rate of per capita income growth. An increase in labor force participation could, however, raise the growth of per capita GDP.

15. A is correct. Klymchuk is referring to the concept of club convergence. The basic premise is that lower-income members of the club are converging to the income levels of the richest countries. This implies that the countries with the lowest per capita income in the club grow at the fastest rate. Countries outside the club, however, continue to fall behind.

16. A is the correct choice. Amaral's initiative to implement a new dividend tax is likely to impede inflows of equity capital by making equity investment in Brazil less attractive for foreign investors. Capital flows, or lack thereof, have a major impact on economic growth because, in an open economy, world savings can finance domestic investment. As a potential source of funds, foreign investment breaks the vicious cycle of low income, low domestic savings, and low investment.

17. A is correct. Mantri's proposal to sponsor a patent initiative, which is likely to result in technology investment and improvement, is likely to cause a proportional upward shift in the entire production function, allowing the economy to produce higher output per worker for a given level of capital per worker. Technological progress also increases the marginal product of capital relative to its marginal cost.

18. C is correct. Maintaining a low currency exchange rate is a policy aimed at maintaining demand for the country's exports. It would have little direct impact on the potential growth rate of aggregate supply. It might boost long-term capacity growth indirectly, however, by encouraging adoption of leading-edge technology. Nonetheless, it would not be expected to be as powerful as capital deepening or investment in technology.

19. A is the correct choice. Kanté's decision to invest in equities in India is supported by the country's strong economic growth. For global investors, economic growth is important since equity composite valuations depend to a great extent on both the level of economic output (GDP per capita and GDP overall) and the rate of economic growth. Relative to Brazil, India's growth rate in per capita GDP has been much higher, and furthermore, its growth rate in GDP has also been much higher than that of Brazil. In contrast to the growth rate, the relatively low *level* of GDP per capita in India is less likely to indicate attractive equity investment opportunities. Low per capita GDP suggests that India may lack sufficient industrial and financial infrastructure to support some types of industries. It also indicates that domestic purchasing power is relatively limited, decreasing the potential for higher-margin, domestically oriented businesses.

20. A is the correct choice. With Mali's low standard of living (i.e., GDP per capita) and large informal workforce, the tax rate is unlikely to be an impediment to growth, so lowering the tax rate is not likely to be a major contributor to growth.

21. B is correct. The strategy for Mali to impose high tariffs (trade restrictions) on imports is likely to undermine rather than enhance growth and therefore is not supportive of convergence with developed economies. Freer trade (fewer trade restrictions) tends to enhance growth by, for example, inducing a shift of resources into industries in which the country has a comparative advantage, thereby increasing overall productivity; forcing less efficient domestic companies to exit and more efficient ones to innovate; allowing domestic producers to more fully exploit economies of scale by selling to a larger market; and enabling less advanced sectors of an economy to catch up with more advanced countries or sectors through knowledge spillovers.

CHAPTER 12

ECONOMICS OF REGULATION

SOLUTIONS

1. A is correct. The Dodd-Frank Act, enacted by the U.S. Congress and signed into law, is an example of a statute (a law enacted by a legislative body).

2. C is correct. The Financial Industry Regulatory Authority (FINRA) is a self-regulatory organization (SRO) and an independent regulator. The chapter states that it describes itself as "the largest independent regulator for all securities firms doing business in the United States. Our chief role is to protect investors by maintaining the fairness of the U.S. capital markets." FINRA oversees over 4,000 brokerage firms, 160,000 branch offices and 629,000 registered securities representatives. FINRA has, as noted by the chapter, "a degree of official sanction but is not a government agency per se." FINRA is referred to specifically in the chapter as an SRO.

3. B is correct. U.S. firms are likely to be concerned due to the earlier timing of the application of more stringent regulations in the United States than in other G-20 countries, as some business may flow to less stringent regulatory environments or jurisdictions.

4. A is the correct choice. Blackout periods are established by *companies* in response to concerns about insider trading. Thus, blackout periods are not a tool used by government to intervene in the financial services sector. Capital requirements are utilized by government regulators to reduce systemic risk and financial contagion. Insider trading restrictions are used by regulators concerned about insiders using their greater knowledge to the disadvantage of others; insider trading restrictions respond to informational frictions.

5. A is correct. The hiring of more lawyers to deal with compliance is an example of an unintended implementation cost. Establishing legal standards for contracts and employers' rights and responsibilities are objectives (intended consequences) of some regulation.

6. A is correct. Regulation Q set a ceiling on the interest rates paid by banks for various types of deposits, which resulted in investors' shifting funds to money market funds.

 CFA Institute

ABOUT THE CFA PROGRAM

The Chartered Financial Analyst (CFA) designation is a globally recognized standard of excellence for measuring the competence and integrity of investment professionals. To earn the CFA charter, candidates must successfully pass through the CFA Program, a global graduate-level self-study program that combines a broad curriculum with professional conduct requirements as preparation for a wide range of investment specialties.

Anchored by a practice-based curriculum, the CFA Program is focused on the knowledge identified by professionals as essential to the investment decision-making process. This body of knowledge maintains current relevance through a regular, extensive survey of practicing CFA charterholders across the globe. The curriculum covers 10 general topic areas, ranging from equity and fixed-income analysis to portfolio management to corporate finance—all with a heavy emphasis on the application of ethics in professional practice. Known for its rigor and breadth, the CFA Program curriculum highlights principles common to every market so that professionals who earn the CFA designation have a thoroughly global investment perspective and a profound understanding of the global marketplace.

www.cfainstitute.org

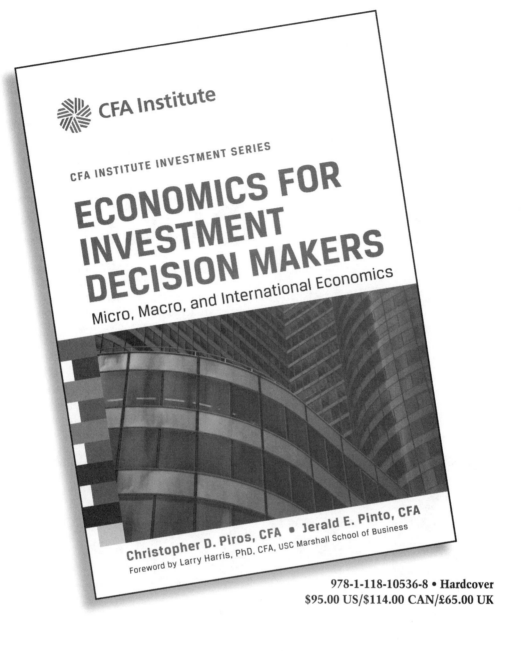

978-1-118-10536-8 • Hardcover
$95.00 US/$114.00 CAN/£65.00 UK

The **tool of choice** for investment decision makers.

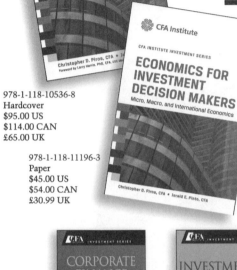

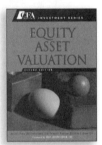

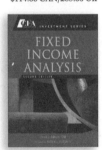
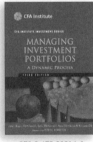